Future Power Now

Future Power Now

Prayer in the Kingdom

Gary Waldecker

Future Power Now: Prayer in the Kingdom
Cover Art by Aaron Rushing
Copyright © 2022 by Gary T. Waldecker

Printed in the United States of America
First Printing, 2023
ISBN 979–8-9882539-0-7
Long Road Press
www.longroadpress.com

For Phyllis
My Most Excellent Partner in Prayer

Table of Contents

Preface

Are you and your church on a mission or do you just support foreign missionaries? To what extent is prayer not just a church activity but a vital part of that mission for you and your church? How important is the presence of Christ's future kingdom to your prayers? Of all the things that excite you, is this one of them?

My primary goal[1] in this book is to promote the excitement of the mission to which God has called the church, and the role of prayer within that mission. The Old Testament promised great future blessing accompanied by the outpouring the Spirit of God. Even though the fullness of that blessing is in our future—at the second coming of Christ—the power of that future kingdom is ours to use now because the Spirit has been poured out and Jesus has begun his reign from heaven. The Bible reveals prayer to be a powerful link between the first and the final stages of the kingdom. It is a weapon of war employed by audacious and bold secret agents on a mission to advance God's kingdom toward its final stage. Through their prayers, kingdom agents bring the transforming power of the future to bear on the present, and thus move the present closer to the future. We have future power now.

When Elisha's servant was afraid, Elisha prayed that the servant would see the reality that was otherwise unseen. He said to the servant,

> "Do not fear, for those who *are* with us *are* more than those who *are* with them." And Elisha prayed, and said, "Lord, I pray, open his eyes that he may see." Then the Lord opened the eyes of the young man, and he saw. And behold, the mountain *was* full of horses and chariots of fire all around Elisha.
> 2 Kings 6:16-17 NKJV

The normally invisible armies of heaven became visible to bolster the faith of the servant. This event was a mere foretaste of the invisible kingdom of God becoming visible in Christ. Although he has gone into heaven, he as sent the Holy Spirit to be with us. Though we do not yet see the kingdom of God in its full glory, it is even now present and we who believe are its citizens. When we pray as those who are sure of the unseen realities, his kingdom advances. Because of the presence of the future kingdom, we pray even now with the power of the future.

I pray that my attempt to apply Scripture to the area of prayer in the kingdom—even as I try to apply it increasingly in my own life—will be a helpful contribution to your prayer life and to that of your church as you engage in its mission.

Chapter 1

Pray for the Kingdom

T he typical stereotype of the reason for prayer in our culture is this: when you have a problem and you've run out of other options, then it's time to pray. When some character in a movie prays, you know the situation has become desperate. When there is no other recourse to solve a problem, prayer is the only option left. When your own ability to solve problems comes to an end, then you've got to ask God. Most Christians I know don't believe this is how prayer should be used. But too many of us act as if we did. Many Christians pray only when the situation seems either astonishingly good or astonishingly bad.

The Locus of Astonishment

Where does your culture locate the source of astonishing things? From a biblical point of view, what kinds of things *should* astonish us? What kinds of things tend to astonish you? The answer to these questions may shed light on how you pray.

The Circumstantial Perspective

The twelve disciples were plagued with what I call the *circum-*

1

stantial perspective. They were astonished by extremely good or extremely unfavorable circumstances more than they were astonished by the coming of the kingdom in Christ. That is, they had misplaced the proper locus of astonishment. They were astonished at the wrong things.

Although the word "astonish" does not appear in Luke 13:1-5, the idea is clearly present. Some Jews told Jesus about a recent shocking tragedy in which some Galileans who had gone to offer sacrifices had been brutally put to death by Pilate. Their assumption was that these people must have been very bad to have suffered such a catastrophe. Bad things like this happen only to very bad people. For these Jews who were amazed at the tragedy, the locus of astonishment had to do with favorable or unfavorable circumstances. The crucial problem in life was misdiagnosed. We might call this misdiagnosis a false problematic. According to this perspective there are two kinds of people, with a "great divide" between them: those who have mostly favorable circumstances and those who don't. It's astonishing, in this view, how such terrible circumstances can happen to some people. This view is illustrated in Figure 1.

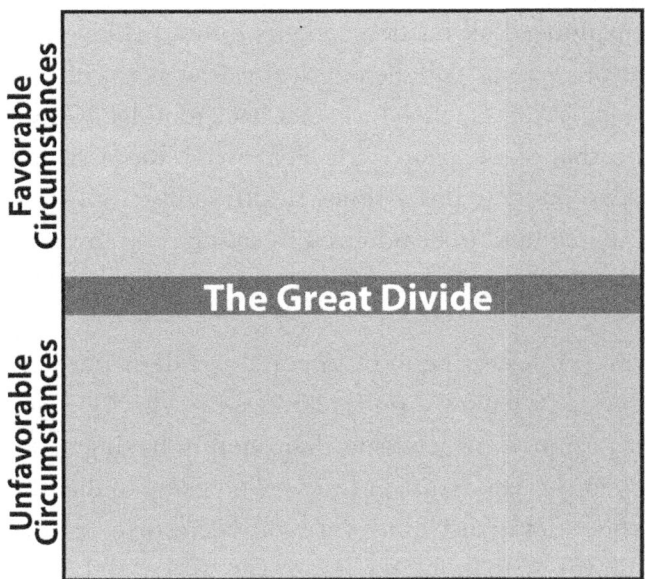

Figure 1. The Locus of Astonishment according to the
Circumstantial Perspective

The Kingdom Perspective

Jesus, on the other hand, was amazed and astonished by the lack of faith among the people of Israel. To the Jews who had told him about this tragedy perpetuated by Pilate, Jesus answered:

> And Jesus said to them, "Do you suppose that these Galileans were greater sinners than all other Galileans because they suffered this fate? I tell you, no, but unless you repent, you will all likewise perish. Or do you suppose that those eighteen on whom the tower in Siloam fell and killed them were worse culprits than all the men who live in Jerusalem? I tell you, no, but unless you repent, you will all likewise perish."
> Luke 13:2-5 NASB 1995

Given the rebellion of Adam and the sin of his descendants, we should be astonished that anyone is still standing and even has the opportunity to repent. Because Adam was the head of the human

3

race, his sin plunged all his descendants into rebellion against God. And that means we must all die physically as well as suffer God's just judgment against rebels when he comes back to judge the world.

It's true that some people are able to accumulate many good circumstances—money, possessions, health and so on. It's also true that these people tend to be admired by others. But in the end, what good does it do when you die? The circumstantial perspective is very short-sighted.

According to Jesus, the most important issue is not having good circumstances, but having a right relationship with God. Jesus came to deal with a much bigger issue than merely having good circumstances. If you put your trust in Jesus—who came to die in the place of those who would trust him—you will be resurrected after death and live forever with him! So Jesus was astonished at the short-sighted lack of faith among the people of his hometown.

> Jesus said to them, "A prophet is not without honor except in his hometown and among his own relatives and in his own household." And He could do no miracle there except that He laid His hands on a few sick people and healed them. And He wondered at their unbelief.
> Mark 6:4-6 NASB 1995

Jesus was also astonished at a Gentile with more faith than his own people.

> But the centurion said, "Lord, I am not worthy for You to come under my roof, but just say the word, and my servant will be healed. For I also am a man under authority, with soldiers under me; and I say to this one, 'Go!' and he goes, and to another, 'Come!' and he comes, and to my slave, 'Do this!' and he does it." Now when Jesus heard this, He marveled and said to those who were following, "Truly I say to you, I have not found such great faith with anyone in Israel.

Matthew 8:8-10 NASB 1995

When Mark summarizes Jesus' ministry and what it means to have faith in God, he frames it in terms of the promised kingdom of God that had been foreshadowed in the Old Testament. He describes the coming of the kingdom as "gospel" or "good news." He says,

> Now after John had been taken into custody, Jesus came into Galilee, preaching the gospel of the kingdom of God[1], and saying, "The time is fulfilled, and the kingdom of God is at hand; repent and believe in the gospel."
> Mark 1:14-15 NKJV

Jesus confirms this when, citing his casting out of demons as evidence, he says,

> .... the kingdom of God has come upon you.
> Luke 11:20 NASB 1995

Jesus had brought very good news— the kingdom of God foreshadowed in the Old Testament had arrived! The coming of the kingdom meant that Jesus came to destroy the devil, deal with sin, and offer eternal life to those who put their trust in him and not in good circumstances. He would do this through his death to pay for the sins of his people, and through his resurrection to conquer the evil one and his grip on people. He came to forgive and give eternal life to those who trust him.

In spite of all this, people didn't seem to care. They were more interested in having good circumstances in the moment. They were very short-sighted and missed the big and more important picture: sin and death and how God's kingdom was going to deal with these.

Figure 2 below illustrates Jesus' perspective. For him, the great divide in life is not between having good circumstances and having bad circumstances. Rather, it's between living as a citizen of the kingdom of God or living as a citizen of the domain of darkness. In practice, this amounts to trusting in God to deliver you from eternal death no matter what your circumstances on the one hand, or trusting yourself to accumulate good circumstances as a citizen of the domain of darkness on the other.

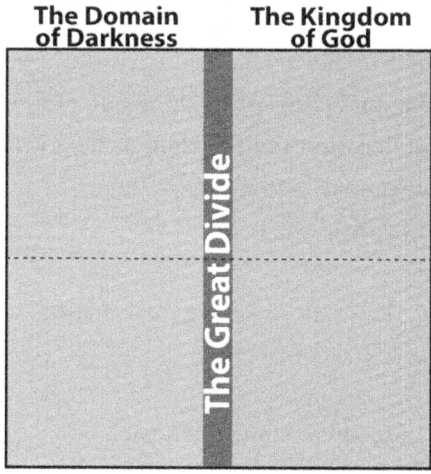

Figure 2. The Locus of Astonishment from Jesus' Point of View

As we have seen, Figure 1 above shows that the disciples had misplaced the locus of astonishment, locating the great divide in life between favorable and unfavorable circumstances. The disciples had heard Jesus main message: the good news of the kingdom. But they were caught up in the false problematic that makes good circumstances versus bad circumstances the framework of their thoughts, prayers and actions. They were more concerned about having good circumstances and avoiding bad ones than they were about the king and his kingdom.

The disciples even interpreted the coming of the kingdom through the lens of the circumstantial perspective. Think of some of the things the disciples asked of Jesus:

1. When are you going to restore the kingdom? (Overthrow the Romans and return us to the glorious days of the past?)
2. Can my son sit on your right hand in the kingdom? (Give us more glory than others).
3. Let's build three shelters. (This glorious moment on the mountain is what we've been looking for. Can we hold onto it now and avoid the pain we've been going through?)
4. Can we call fire down from heaven now on these unbelievers? (We are the good guys and we've got Jesus, so we deserve good things and not judgment like these bad people.)

These requests are in some ways all related to God's kingdom. But they are all over-focused on the good circumstances that the kingdom would bring instead of on the king himself. For all practical purposes, the disciples interpreted the kingdom through the lens of the circumstantial perspective. It's easy to fall into the trap of using kingdom language while really asking for our own kingdom that's filled only with good and comfortable circumstances.

So, the question we need to ask ourselves is this: To what extent do we long for the king and his kingdom? How does our desire for the kingdom compare to our desire for good circumstances? If someone were to observe your daily actions, what would be their conclusion? How excited are you about the kingdom? To help us answer these questions, let's take a closer look at the King, the kingdom and its citizens.

The King, the Kingdom and its Citizens

The kingdom of God is the rule of king Jesus in heaven and earth[2]. Jesus told his disciples:

All authority in heaven and earth has been given to me.
Matthew 28:18 NASB 1995

In other words, on the basis of Jesus' death and resurrection he is now the human[3] king of the world.[4] Whoever conquers death—and that's what Jesus did by rising from the dead into eternal life—is by default the king. Furthermore, Jesus came as the Second Adam—designated by the Father as the second and final head of the human race. Just as Adam represented the human race and sealed us as rebels against God when he decided to sin, so Jesus represents the human race[5] when he brings his kingdom.[6] This means that the life of everyone is in Jesus' hands. Everyone will appear before this king in the final judgment.

Before this turning point in history—the coming of the kingdom in Jesus—demons ruled the world[7] except among God's people Israel. Even among them, however, demons all too often had more influence than they should have because of ungodly human kings. The Bible calls the rule of demons over humanity the "domain of darkness."[8] Demons typically exercise their rule by tempting people to focus on good circumstances so in the end they can eat you for lunch. As Peter says:

Your adversary, the devil, prowls around like a roaring lion, seeking someone to devour.
1 Peter 5:8b NASB 1995

Imagine being a prisoner of war in enemy territory. Now imagine the whole human race being there willingly rather than submit to God. That's the domain of darkness. Furthermore, according to the Bible, there is no one who—based on his own record—will be able to avoid eternal punishment. The apostle Paul makes this clear when he says:

There is no righteous person, not even one; There is no one who understands, There is no one who seeks out God; They have all turned aside, together they have become corrupt; There is no one who does good, There is not even one.

Romans 3:11-12 NASB 1995

Having conquered death, King Jesus offers to rescue people from the domain of darkness[9] with its fear of death and the tyranny of the devil.[10] All we need to do is accept his generous terms of surrender.[11] As Jesus' human enemies—and that's the whole human race—do accept these terms of surrender through repentance and faith, he rescues us from the domain of darkness and moves us into his kingdom.[12] Figure 3 illustrates this transfer. The apostle Paul says of those who have put their trust in Christ,

He rescued us from the domain of darkness, and transferred us to the kingdom of His beloved Son, in whom we have redemption, the forgiveness of sins.

Colossians 1:13-14 NASB 1995

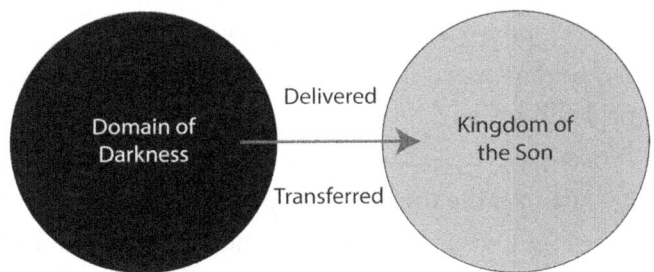

Figure 3. Delivered from one Domain to another

The word "domain" could also be properly translated "authority." The evil one—as a result of the fall—has become "the god of this age."[13] As such, he exercises authority over all people who have not been transferred out of his domain. Those who have been delivered and transferred are no longer under his authority but under the authority of Christ the king.

There are movies and television shows about people moving among parallel dimensions. In these stories, travelers often find different versions of themselves in different dimensions. While these parallel dimensions do not exist, the idea is a distortion of something that is indeed true. The Bible talks about two dimensions:[14] the domain of darkness and the kingdom of Christ. As believers we are citizens of the latter, but have a mission to complete among those who still belong to the former. We are involved with two dimensions at the same time.[15] As people are moved into his kingdom through repentance and faith, God's will is increasingly done on earth as it is always done in heaven.[16]

When you are transferred by God's grace into the kingdom of his Son Jesus Christ, your identity is no longer found in your gifts, abilities, possessions, or anything else in this world. It is found in your relationship to Christ. Katie[17] claimed to be a Christian and was also the star of the women's volleyball team of her Christian high school. While she claimed to be a Christian, in practice, she found her sense of identity and worth in her ability to play volleyball and in the praise she received from others for being so good at it. When she injured herself in a way that prevented her from continuing to play volleyball, her world fell apart. She became bitter and angry at God, and this lasted for several years. Eventually she began to view her injury in light of eternity and the unseen reality of God's kingdom. She realized that her sense of worth and identity had been wrapped up in her giftedness and the praise she received from others. She began to understand the amazing value of being forgiven, given a new identity as a child of God, and the promise of living forever. She repented of her bitterness and began to rejoice in her status as a citizen of the kingdom.

Swept up into the Story

The Bible is much more than a collection of truths for living. It is the greatest story of all time, and we God's people have been given the privilege of participating in it as significant actors. The most exciting movie or book can't compare with this story—and stories are good to the extent that they honor the themes of this one. It's the multifaceted story about the Son of God who was destined to be the King of the human race. His bride-to-be was tempted away by the villain who wanted the throne of the Son as well as his bride. She believed his lies and rebelled against the King. But the Son rescued her through his own death.

His death wasn't the end, though, because he conquered death by rising to a higher state of life. The story continues! Having been raised from the dead and having empowered his people with the presence of the Holy Spirit, the Son is even now working through his bride to bring out all the implications of his victory in preparation for his coming again as the glorious conquering hero.

If you are a believer in Jesus, you have been swept up into this true unfolding story. To what extent have you become aware of what that means? To what extent has Jesus become your hero at whose side you are engaged in the story? Or are you still trying to be the hero of your own story? As for me, I'm still learning what it all means, but eagerly so!

Kingdom Blessing and Suffering Together

Learning what it means to be in the kingdom is challenging because it hasn't come in the way most people expected. God's people in the Old Testament expected the kingdom to bring an unprecedented time of blessing in which there would be no suffering. They divided history into two main parts: *This Age* and *The Age to Come*. They expected *This Age* to come to an end, and to be replaced by the *Age to Come*, to be ruled by the Messianic son of David, as shown in

Figure 4. They expected the kind of blessing that we will see only after the second coming of Christ.

Figure 4. The Expectation of God's People in the Old
Testament

In the New Testament we see clearly what was not so clear before: that the promised kingdom comes in three phases: its inauguration, its progress, and its consummation. The kingdom was inaugurated by Christ at his first coming. He himself was glorified and entered the final stage of the kingdom through his resurrection and ascension into heaven. He is already experiencing what our future will be at his second coming when we will enter into that full experience of the kingdom.

In the meantime, he has given us a foretaste of the blessings of the future kingdom by pouring out the Holy Spirit. We live in the period of progress often called the "Now-But-Not-Yet." That is, the kingdom is really here *now*. Furthermore, it is growing and will continue to increase.[18] It will arrive in its fulness at the second coming of Christ. We have been given a very real foretaste and growing experience of the blessings and power of the future.

At the same time, we continue to see sin and evil affecting our daily lives. People still suffer the consequences of sin. This Age, characterized by sin, pain, suffering and death, continues on even though the kingdom has come. Or we could put it the other way: the glorious future kingdom has partially entered the present before the age of sin and death is over. The two ages overlap each other, as illustrated in Figure 5. As the apostle Paul says, we have this treasure of the good news of the kingdom in jars of clay.[19] That is, we have the glory of the Age to Come through the presence of the Holy Spirit, but we experience that glory in the midst of weakness. In this way it's clear that the power operating in and through us is not from us but from God.

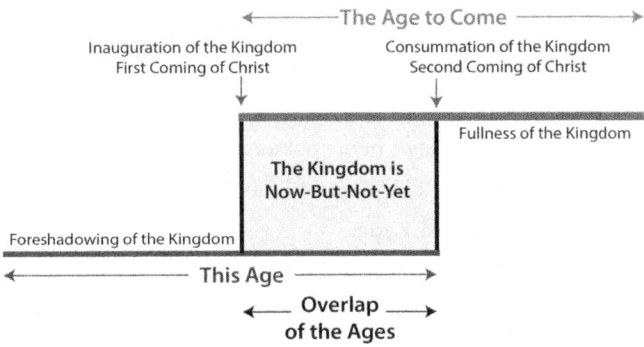

Figure 5. The Overlap of the Ages Results In the Now-But-Not-Yet Kingdom

During this in-between period—the Now-But-Not-Yet—we simultaneously experience the blessings of the kingdom and the suffering that characterizes This Age. The overlap of the ages produces an experiential contradiction that Paul describes this way:

We are afflicted in every way, but not crushed; perplexed, but not despairing; persecuted, but not forsaken; struck down, but not destroyed; always carrying about in the body the dying of Jesus, so that the life of Jesus also may be manifested in our body. For we who live are constantly being delivered over to death for Jesus' sake, so that the life of Jesus also may be manifested in our mortal flesh.....

Therefore we do not lose heart, but though our outer man is decaying, yet our inner man is being renewed day by day. For momentary, light affliction is producing for us an eternal weight of glory far beyond all comparison, while we look not at the things which are seen, but at the things which are not seen; for the things which are seen are temporal, but the things which are not seen are eternal.

2 Corinthians 4:8-11, 16-18 NASB 1995

In fact, the Bible says that in this period we have the *privilege* of suffering for the sake of Christ and his kingdom.

> Blessed are those who have been persecuted for the sake of righteousness, for theirs is the kingdom of heaven.
>
> Matthew 5:10 NASB 1995
>
> If you are reviled for the name of Christ, you are blessed, because the Spirit of glory and of God rests on you. Make sure that none of you suffers as a murderer, or thief, or evildoer, or a troublesome meddler; but if anyone suffers as a Christian, he is not to be ashamed, but is to glorify God in this name.
>
> 1 Peter 4:14-16 NASB 1995
>
> Therefore, those also who suffer according to the will of God shall entrust their souls to a faithful Creator in doing what is right.
>
> 1 Peter 4:19 NASB 1995
>
> For to you it has been granted for Christ's sake, not only to believe in Him, but also to suffer for His sake....
>
> Philippians 1:29 NASB 1995

In the Now-But-Not-Yet kingdom, we experience the blessings of the kingdom and suffering simultaneously. So don't be astonished if you, as a child of God and member of the kingdom, find yourself suffering. That is not the proper locus of astonishment. Rather, we should be astonished by other realities.

The Astonishing Kingdom

When it comes to the issue of circumstances—whether pleasant or threatening—there is something astonishing about the kingdom. Even though we suffer for the sake of the kingdom, we are assured that God is at work in *everything* that happens to us for our good.

And we know that God causes all things to work together for good to those who love God, to those who are called according to His purpose.

    Romans 8:28 NASB 1995

King Jesus has defeated death—and with it every threatening circumstance—through his own death and resurrection. Nothing can harm God's people unless he permits it for his kingdom purposes. Because the kingdom has come in the midst of sin and its effects, we are to live and pray in light of the unseen reality of the kingdom.

The evangelist George Whitfield was used of the Lord mightily in the First Great Awakening. It is estimated that he preached eighteen thousand formal sermons, and many more informal ones. People flocked to hear him preach. But there were others who tried to kill him. After one assassination attempt, he remarked, "We are immortal until our work on earth is done."[20] Indeed, believers walk with a protective shield around us:

But You, O Lord, are a shield about me, My glory, and the One who lifts my head.

    Psalm 3:3 NASB 1995

Because of this protective shield, only those difficult circumstances that he allows for his good kingdom purposes can touch us.

But the Lord does use both pleasant and threatening circumstances to bring forward his kingdom plan. It's part of the adventure. Imagine watching an action/adventure movie in which the hero suffers no challenges, no setbacks, no difficult circumstances. I have no doubt you would change the channel and look for something more interesting. So, it is in this greatest adventure of all time into which we as God's people have been caught up: we experience all kinds of challenging and unpleasant circumstances. But the Lord is at work in all of them for the good of his people and the progress of his kingdom. In that ultimate sense, all circumstances the Lord allows in our lives are favorable. We will look at this adventure in more detail in chapter 3.

If you are a believer in Christ, no doubt your experience is similar to mine in this regard. As I look back on my life I can now see how again and again I found myself in painful circumstances that made me cry out, "Why are you letting this happen to me? Where are your promises? What does this have to do with the kingdom?" And again, and again I have seen the Lord working through them to accomplish various kingdom purposes: to reveal my weaknesses, to help me grow and become a more effective kingdom agent, to reveal how God can do things through weak people in difficult circumstances, to teach us what he can do through our faith, to move his kingdom forward.

This means that the main issue in the kingdom is not suffering versus happiness. The main issue is not whether we have good circumstances or unfavorable ones[21]. Ultimately in the consummated kingdom we look forward to good circumstances with no suffering.[22] But for now we live with both. The main issue now is the presence and progress of the kingdom. Are you still in the domain of darkness? Or have you been transferred by grace into the kingdom? If you have been thus relocated, what difference does it make in your life? What difference does it make in your prayers?

Implications for Prayer

Our prayers should be oriented around this one:

> Your kingdom come!
> Matthew 6:10 NASB 1995

We also pray for our daily bread. But this is food we need in order to serve in the kingdom.[23]

Every church member I know would agree with me on this--in theory anyway. However, most prayer meetings,[24] it seems to me, have been at least partially captivated by the circumstantial frame of reference. Here's my evidence: the content of most prayers I hear consists of (1) asking God for favorable circumstances, (2) asking him to take away or otherwise deal with unfavorable circumstances, and (3) praising God for favorable circumstances. Sometimes I hear qualifiers--like "if it be your will"--that soften the circumstantial perspective to some extent. Once in a while you might actually hear some passion for the full coming of the kingdom and a request relating to circumstances in that light. But for the most part, the circumstantial perspective is there to one degree or another and typically dominates.

I don't want to overstate my case. God *is* concerned about our circumstances. He is deeply compassionate when we suffer. On one occasion he had compassion on the multitudes just because they were hungry and had come a long distance:

> In those days, when there was again a large crowd and they had nothing to eat, Jesus called His disciples and said to them, "I feel compassion for the people because they have remained with Me now three days and have nothing to eat. If I send them away hungry to their homes, they will faint on the way; and some of them have come from a great distance."
> Mark 8:1-3 NASB 1995

He *does* answer prayers for help in difficult circumstances. He has a special concern for the poor and afflicted. While God's people are called to be concerned about the progress of the kingdom, they are also beloved children of the Father and the bride of Christ. However, such compassion is never divorced from God's kingdom plan and concerns and should not be coopted into the circumstantial perspective. The great divide in life is not between good circumstances and bad circumstances. We are not to find our sense of worth in good circumstances or find life meaningless to the extent that we don't have them. We are citizens of the kingdom!

Sometimes when people pray for good circumstances and to be delivered from bad ones, they have an unexpressed and implicit kingdom perspective. Although they may not state it, they have in the back of their minds something like this: "I pray for healing because I want to see your kingdom come and I believe my gifts can still be useful in this or that way to promote the coming of the kingdom."[25] In other words, in their minds the desire for good circumstances has not become more important than Christ and his kingdom. This is still a kingdom-oriented prayer. I think it would be helpful to make it more explicitly kingdom-oriented.

On the other hand, I find the circumstantial perspective pressing itself with force into the prayer life of many churches. One way to combat this tendency is to be more intentionally thoughtful about our motives and reasons. As you pray for this or that change of circumstance, ask yourself *why* you are making this request. For example, if you ask the group for prayer for your uncle who isn't feeling well this week, first ask yourself *why* you want the Lord to make him feel better. Someone might respond, "Well, isn't having compassion on someone who is suffering enough?" Yes, there's a sense in which it is. But even compassion should not be divorced from the kingdom. So, as you pray, make your reasons explicit.

A focus on the kingdom and the King will rescue us from the circumstantial perspective. As Martin Luther says in his hymn "A Mighty Fortress is our God,"

> Let goods and kindred go, this mortal life also; the body they may
> kill: God's truth abideth still; His kingdom is forever.

Understanding by faith the reality that in Christ the kingdom of God has come and is coming frames everything differently. Of course, it's not wrong to pray for the sick or for those who need a job or for protection from harm. We *should* pray for these things. And sooner or later the Lord will wipe away the tears. But if these things are continually and almost exclusively the only kinds of prayers you hear from a group, what does that say about their desire for the full coming of the kingdom? These requests for alleviation of discomfort need to be framed at least implicitly within a kingdom perspective in which the most astonishing things are not good and bad circumstances.

God is much more interested in the progress of his kingdom than he is in our comfort. He is much more interested in our effectiveness as kingdom agents than he is in protecting us from unfavorable circumstances. The full coming of his kingdom--whether through favorable or unfavorable circumstances--is his mission. And that's how we should pray even if it means we suffer. Your kingdom come!

Follow-up

1. As a believer in Christ, in what ways have you become aware of having been swept up into the greatest adventure of all time? If you have little awareness of this, pray that the Lord would open your understanding to see the great things he has done for you and the great things he has for you to do in his kingdom adventure.

2. How would you explain the difference between being caught in the circumstantial perspective and praying with compassion for those who have problems? Make an effort to avoid falling into the circumstantial perspective as you pray.

3. Examine your prayers. Would it be clear to those who hear you pray that you are concerned about the full coming of the kingdom? Would it be clear that you are not primarily asking for good circumstances? Give your evidence. Work at making this ever clearer.

4. When you pray for someone's good health, or that they get a job, have you examined your reasons and motives for these requests? Why are you typically making those

requests? Think through your reasons for the requests you make.

5. How many people attend the prayer meeting in your church? What percentage of the total membership is this? How do you evaluate that attendance number? What do you think it would take for more people to attend? Is there anything you can do about it?

6. Do you attend—or have you attended—the prayer meetings of your church? Why or why not?

7. How would you describe the prayer meetings in your church? How much time is spent actually praying? If unbelievers were present, do you think they would feel how important the full coming of the kingdom is to your church? Provide evidence for your answer.

Chapter 2

Pray as a Kingdom Agent

I was listening intently to the sermon. The preacher was talking about prayer. At a certain point in the sermon he said something like the following:

> Since God is sovereign and already has everything planned out, our prayers don't really change anything. Prayer doesn't change anything, but it's good for us. You might say it changes us, making us more submissive to God's will.

Even though I have a firm belief in God's sovereignty, I felt myself react emotionally and even physically to what the preacher was saying. I have always believed that prayer is more than an exercise in sanctification. So what do *you* think? Does prayer really change anything? Since God is sovereign and already has his plan in place, what difference does prayer really make?

One of the interesting things about the Bible is that it presents a God who is sovereign and who at the same time gives his people a significant role in the full coming of his kingdom. In other words, we are his kingdom agents[1]. "Agent" is often defined in these two ways:

(1) a person who acts on behalf of another person, and (2) someone who takes an active role in bringing about a specified effect. Christ has inaugurated the kingdom and has made his people active agents who work on his behalf toward its full coming. To the extent that God works in and through us to bring about his kingdom purposes, we should act and pray as kingdom agents.

The Significance of Agent Actions

God is sovereign and has planned everything that happens. This is clear from many passages of Scripture. For example,

> In Him also we have obtained an inheritance, having been predestined according to His purpose who works all things after the counsel of His will....
> Ephesians 1:10b-11 NASB 1995

However, deducing from this statement that our role is passive or insignificant does not do justice to Scripture[2]. The Westminster Confession of Faith deals with the relationship between God's sovereignty and mankind's responsibility. Look at the following sections:

> God from all eternity, did, by the most wise and holy counsel of His own will, freely, and unchangeably ordain whatsoever comes to pass; yet so, as thereby neither is God the author of sin, nor is violence offered to the will of the creatures; nor is the liberty or contingency of second causes taken away, but rather established. WCF 3.1
> Although, in relation to the foreknowledge and decree of God, the first Cause, all things come to pass immutably, and infallibly; yet, by the same providence, He orders them to fall out, according to the nature of second causes, either necessarily, freely, or contingently. WCF 5.2
> God, in His ordinary providence, makes use of means, yet is

free to work without, above, and against them, at His pleasure. WCF 5.3

According to these paragraphs, everything that happens is part of God's plan. On the other hand, God has chosen for the most part to use secondary causes— like the laws of physics, apparently random events[3], and the actions of people—in the working out of his plan. Someone who says, "It doesn't matter what I do because it's all going to turn out according to God's plan in the end anyway," does not believe in the Biblical doctrine of sovereignty, but in fatalism[4]. What we do matters and has consequences. How and whether we pray also has consequences. As James says,

> You do not have because you do not ask. You ask and do not receive, because you ask with wrong motives, so that you may spend it on your pleasures.
> James 4:2b-3 NASB 1995

The story of Joseph shows us how the Bible views the relationship between God's sovereignty and our responsibility. Joseph's brothers had sold him into slavery. Much later they found he was the second in command in Egypt and held their lives in his hands. How would he treat them? Would he take revenge? Joseph alleviated their fears when he said,

> As for you, you meant evil against me, but God meant it for good in order to bring about this present result, to preserve many people alive.
> Genesis 50:20 NASB 1995

Regarding the one event of Joseph being sold into slavery, there were two actors: the brothers and God. The event was 100% an act of God, as well as 100% an act of the brothers. These two actors had two different motives: the brothers had evil motives while God had good motives. God did not obligate the brothers to sin, nor is he guilty of their sin. The brothers are guilty, even though it was also an act of God.

We see something similar when God used Assyria to punish his own people.

Woe to Assyria, the rod of My anger and the staff in whose hands is My indignation, I send it against a godless nation and commission it against the people of My fury to capture booty and to seize plunder, and to trample them down like mud in the streets. Yet it does not so intend, nor does it plan so in its heart, but rather it is its purpose to destroy and to cut off many nations. For it says, "Are not my princes all kings? "As my hand has reached to the kingdoms of the idols, whose graven images were greater than those of Jerusalem and Samaria.... Shall I not do to Jerusalem and her images just as I have done to Samaria and her idols?" So it will be that when the Lord has completed all His work on Mount Zion and on Jerusalem, He will say, "I will punish the fruit of the arrogant heart of the king of Assyria and the pomp of his haughtiness".... Is the axe to boast itself over the one who chops with it? Is the saw to exalt itself over the one who wields it? That would be like a club wielding those who lift it, or like a rod lifting him who is not wood.

Isaiah 10:5-8, 10-12, 15 NASB 1995

The king of Assyria is like a rod or an axe in God's hand. Through Assyria God will punish his wayward people. However, after he does this, he will punish the king of Assyria for having done it. Here again we have one event with two actors. The event was 100% an act of God. It was also 100% an act of the king of Assyria. God's motives were righteous, while the king of Assyria was proud. The king of Assyria must be punished for invading God's people because of his pride. Yet God righteously used him to carry out his own just judgments.

The crucifixion of Jesus provides another clear example:

.... this Man, delivered over by the predetermined plan and fore-
knowledge of God, you nailed to a cross by the hands of godless
men and put Him to death.

Acts 2:23 NASB 1995

Again, we have one event—the crucifixion of Jesus—and two
actors. It was 100% an act of God. It was also 100% an act of people.
Those who crucified Jesus were guilty of great sin. At the same time,
it was an act of God through which he satisfied his just judgment
against his people.

In these examples, the human actor(s) acted sinfully. In the
following example we see the importance and significance of our
decisions when they are not sinful.

So Saul summoned all the people for war, to go down to Keilah to
besiege David and his men. Now David knew that Saul was plot-
ting evil against him; so he said to Abiathar the priest, "Bring the
ephod here." Then David said, "O Lord God of Israel, Your
servant has heard for certain that Saul is seeking to come to Keilah
to destroy the city on my account. Will the men of Keilah
surrender me into his hand? Will Saul come down just as Your
servant has heard? O Lord God of Israel, I pray, tell Your servant."
And the Lord said, "He will come down." Then David said, "Will
the men of Keilah surrender me and my men into the hand of
Saul?" And the Lord said, "They will surrender you." Then David
and his men, about six hundred, arose and departed from Keilah,
and they went wherever they could go. When it was told Saul that
David had escaped from Keilah, he gave up the pursuit.

1 Samuel 23:8-13 NASB 1995

Our decisions make a difference. If David had stayed in Keilah,
he would have been handed over to Saul. He didn't stay and was

delivered from Saul. Of course, it was part of God's eternal plan that David should leave. On the other hand, David had a legitimate choice before him.

We may find it difficult intellectually to completely reconcile God's sovereignty and our responsibility as kingdom agents. But Scripture teaches both, and both truths require unambiguous responses of faith and obedience. So, although we may have a hard time understanding how they fit together, we do know how to respond in faith and obedience to each doctrine. For example, because he is sovereign, we trust him. Because we are responsible, we obey him. Because God has decided to bring in the fullness of the kingdom through his Spirit-empowered people, if we don't evangelize those the Lord has placed in our path, they will not be saved. On the other hand, because God is sovereign and has chosen a multitude of people to be saved, he will carry out his plans to save the elect through others who are willing agents. Furthermore, we will find that this was part of God's eternal plan, but we ourselves will miss out on advancing the mission and the reward that we could have had. And it will be our own fault.

We can look at prayer the same way. If we don't pray, we shouldn't expect the Lord to use us to advance his great mission. But our lack of prayer doesn't frustrate God's eternal plan. We will find that it was part of his plan to use the prayers of others to move his kingdom forward. We will miss out on the mission and the reward. And it will be our own fault.

Many churches have been infected by what I call "sovereign-itis," which I define as the inflammation of our belief in God's sovereignty in a way that tends to minimize our Biblical responsibility to get involved in his kingdom work. Most people from such churches would not deny that we have some degree of responsibility, but they tend to minimize this teaching. For example, they would agree that we should obey God, pray, and go to church. But they would probably see going out of our way to bring forward God's kingdom purposes as taking things into our own hands. They would tend to minimize the efficacy of prayer. They think, "Since God is sovereign, prayer doesn't really change anything. It's just something God wants us to do. It's for our own benefit." They assume that if God wants to save people, or help them grow, or show them his love, he will somehow do it without much initiative from us. They seem to have the idea that if God wants them to take initiative as kingdom agents, he will hit them over the head with some providential opportunity so clear that no one could miss it. So, if someone comes knocking at your door wanting to know how to be saved, only then do you spring into action. These are not eager and proactive kingdom agents, but reluctant and reactive ones.

God created Adam and Eve as rulers over creation under his own authority as the Great King. God has always given his people a significant role in his kingdom purposes. This is part of his plan. It gives us an opportunity to imitate his own initiative-taking as people made in his image. He has commissioned us as kingdom agents and our actions have consequences.

Pray With Initiative

Because we are kingdom agents, we should take initiative—within the sphere of God's revealed will—to do the things that move his plan forward. One of the ways we participate in this mission as kingdom agents is by praying in a proactive and specific way for the full coming of the kingdom. When it comes to prayer, we should not be passive or only reactive. We should take initiative. Prayer is an indispensable link between the initial coming of the kingdom and its fullness.[5] God brings in the fullness of his kingdom *through* the prayers of his people. In prayer, God expects us to ask him for--even insist on in the face of huge obstacles like institutional and cultural sin--the consummation of his promises. Prayer is an opportunity for God's people to participate in the greatest mission of all time: the full coming of God's kingdom. For example, Paul says to the believers at Philippi that God will deliver him "through their prayers."[6] There is

27

a sense in which Paul won't be delivered if they don't pray. Their prayers are necessary for his deliverance. He also says,

> Finally, brothers, pray for us, that the word of the Lord may speed ahead and be honored, as happened among you, and that we may be delivered from wicked and evil men. For not all have faith.
> 2 Thessalonians 3:1-2 ESV

The phrase "speed ahead" means to run as in a race. The forces of evil are working as hard as they can to keep people in the grip of their power. But the Word of the Lord can get ahead of this with the result that God's people are delivered from evil men. How does this happen? Through the prayers of God's people. Yes, God is sovereign, but it's also true that our prayers can change things.

Pray as God's Co-Worker

I have come to believe the Lord treats us like friends who are also partners in his kingdom mission. Clearly, he calls his disciples "friends" in John 15:15 based on the fact that he has revealed to them "all that I have heard from the Father." So, since we are his friends, Jesus shares his knowledge with us just as he did with Abraham in Genesis 18:17-19. Also, I find no compelling reason to disagree with John Calvin when he interprets 1 Corinthians 3:9 in this way: "We are God's co-workers."[7] To be sure, we are not equal partners. He is God and we are his dependent people. It's his plan and he involves us in it. But giving us a partner role is part of his plan to have us reflect his glory. He gives us the opportunity to imitate him in his ruling and initiative-taking. So, since we are his friends and partners in this great mission, he shares his knowledge with us, wants us to tell him what we think and desire, and gets us involved with him in it.

When I go to a restaurant, I'm always interested in how the waiters or waitresses explain what they're doing. Recently I've heard a lot of, "I'll be taking care of you today." To me, this communicates

"I'm a professional and I know what you need." What bothers me even more is when they say, "What do we want today," as if they were going to sit down and eat with me. I prefer to hear waiters say something like, "I'll be your server today." This makes me feel like they're interested in knowing what I want. As I reflect on my restaurant experiences, I'm stunned to hear these words from Jesus:

> For who is greater, the one who reclines at the table or the one who serves? Is it not the one who reclines at the table? But I am among you as the one who serves.
> Luke 22:27 NASB 1995

Here Jesus likens himself to someone who serves those who are dining. Jesus is standing at the table, as it were, wanting to know what I would like. There is an important sense in which Jesus, respecting the fact that you are made in the image of God and now recreated in the image of Christ in a way that is uniquely you isn't in this situation telling you what to do[8], but wants you to tell him what is on your mind, and what *you* would like to do.

A good leader of an organization will not normally micromanage. Although he's interested in the details of the work, he does not need or even want to be telling everyone specifically what to do in every situation. Rather, he helps create a unifying vision within which the work should be done. He promotes synergy among the organizational members by valuing, enhancing, and drawing on their experience, abilities, and insights. Instead of using them as pawns to accomplish his goals, instead of telling them specifically what to do in every situation, he engages them as significant players so the organization will thrive from the unique contributions of each as they work together.

Neither does God normally micromanage. He values the gifts, experience, and insights of his people.[9] Viewed from this perspective, prayer becomes vital communication in the fulfillment of God's kingdom plans. Prayer is how we let God know our perspective on what needs to be done in our part of the world to bring forward his kingdom purposes. Of course, he already knows this, but still wants to hear our perspective because he has decided to work through us. Prayer is also a way of thanking him for things like the clear direction he has given through his Word and his providential guidance and care. It's also a way of asking him for wisdom as we face new and challenging situations. It's a way of honoring him for his wisdom, power and love revealed in Christ and in his plans for the church. It's a way of confessing our failures and asking for forgiveness. It's a way of asking for the power of the Spirit as we face otherwise impossible challenges. Since God has decided to work through us his people, and since he treats us with dignity and as having a significant role, prayer is a vital communication link in God's plan to bring in the fullness of his kingdom.

Prayer, then, is a great privilege. By asking us to pray he says, as it were, "I'm interested in what you are doing. Tell me about it. Evaluate your situation. There are so many possibilities before you. What do you think is called for in this context? How are you going to engage your gifts and the power of the Spirit I have given you as you take advantage of this specific opportunity? What creative solutions have you come up with? Which one do you think will work best in this instance? And remember who I am! What help do you need from me?" The proactive kingdom prayers of God's people are indispensable to the progress of the kingdom. Understanding this Biblical perspective on prayer makes it very exciting—although still hard work —as we see just what level of importance God has attached to our role as kingdom agents. Listen as Jesus tells us how much he wants us to be involved in the full coming of his kingdom:

> Whatever you ask in My name, that will I do, so that the Father may be glorified in the Son. If you ask Me anything in My name, I will do it.
>
> John 14:13-14 NASB 1995

These verses make best sense when we remember that God has

made us partners in promoting the full coming of his kingdom. Prayers made in the name of Jesus "are not selfish but in the interest of God's kingdom. They proceed from faith, are in accordance with God's will.... A prayer in Christ's name is a prayer that is in harmony with whatever Christ has revealed concerning himself."[10]

On the one hand God is sovereign and will definitely bring in the fullness of his kingdom. Nothing and no one can frustrate or change his plan. On the other hand, he uses his people as key agents in this process. He expects us to evaluate our various situations and to take appropriate initiative. There's a sense in which, if we do nothing, nothing will get done. If we don't pray, nothing will happen. On the other hand, if we refuse to engage in the battle through prayer, we will find that God has passed over us and has moved his plans forward through others who were more eager to participate as kingdom agents. And we will find that such was God's plan all along. After all, he *is* sovereign, and nothing can thwart his purposes. But you are a kingdom agent. Get engaged!

Pray With a View to Action

If lack of prayer is sometimes a symptom of activism--depending on the gifts the Lord has given us instead of on him—expecting God to answer prayer apart from our gifts can easily lead to a lack of taking seriously the kingdom responsibility the Lord has given us. Normally the Lord answers our prayers through his people: through us! That's why the Lord answers our prayers by giving us his Spirit.

> Now suppose one of you fathers is asked by his son for a fish; he will not give him a snake instead of a fish, will he? Or if he is asked for an egg, he will not give him a scorpion, will he? If you then, being evil, know how to give good gifts to your children, how much more will your heavenly Father give the Holy Spirit to those who ask Him?"
>
> Luke 11:11-13 NASB 1995

The best thing the Father can give us is the Holy Spirit. Anything that comes without the Holy Spirit is not worth having. Jesus died and was raised to life to obtain this wonderful gift for us. Every believer already has the Spirit. But we are to continually ask for the Spirit. There is more! He gives us his Spirit so all the benefits of Christ's death and resurrection are increasingly useful to us. He gives us his Spirit so we can increasingly use our gifts to face the challenges before us. So don't pray and then just sit around expecting the Lord to answer apart from your activity. He may use someone else, and he may answer in conjunction with some providential intervention, but don't count on it. Be open to the possibility that he may want to answer—at least partly—through you and your gifts.

Sometimes the Lord wants to answer through you and your ministry team, but in order for that to happen, you may need to grow--as individuals and/or as a group. So, as you pray, be open to the Lord's leading in this regard. If we're not willing to grow, the Lord may pass over us and use someone else to accomplish his purposes. Struggling in prayer sometimes means struggling through your own fears and pride as you face the challenges before you. I have seen missionary teams fold and give up under such pressure. They would rather give in to the status quo than face their fears and pride in order to be more useful kingdom agents. I myself have faced this challenge and have sometimes failed to press on. But when by grace I have, the Lord has always increased my kingdom influence and usefulness.

Follow-up

1. Do you believe that prayer changes things?
2. Have you seen what I'm calling "sovereign-itis" in your own life and prayers? Give evidence for your answer. If you do see it, how does it manifest itself? Remind

yourself of the fact that in Christ you are a kingdom agent in the greatest mission of all time. What are you going to do about it?

3. Have you seen what I'm calling "sovereign-itis" in the life and prayers of your church? Give evidence for your answer. If you do see it, how does it manifest itself?

4. How do you feel about God treating you as a significant partner in his kingdom plans? Have you prayed this way? If not, how would you characterize your prayers? Give examples one way or the other. What steps can you take to participate in prayer as a kingdom agent with more initiative and with a greater view to action?

5. How do you feel as a believer about being commissioned by God as an agent on a great mission?

6. How do you feel about these statements: "if you don't pray nothing will happen" and "if you don't pray, God may pass over you and use someone else to accomplish his kingdom purposes"?

7. Does knowing that God may want to answer your prayers through you make you more hesitant or less hesitant to pray? Explain your answer.

Chapter 3

Pray as an Adventurer

I enjoy good adventure stories like *The Lord of the Rings* by Tolkien.[1] In that story I particularly like the character of Aragorn—aka Strider—who for a while hid his real identity because it wasn't yet time for the return of the king. In fact, I've always wished I could be a secret agent in some great adventure. As I've gotten older, however, I've realized that wish has come true! The mission on which God sends us as agents is indeed an adventure—in fact, it's the greatest adventure of all time.

Pray as Agents on a Challenging Mission

Through the creation account, God reveals himself as a God of adventure. We see this first of all in the manner in which God created. No doubt he could have created Adam and Eve, the Garden of Eden, and everything else with a single command. Instead, he created in stages. Why would he do it that way? It seems odd. Why did it take him so long? Let's look in more detail how he created in stages in order to see how this method points us to the role of adventure in God's plans.

In the first stage God created "formless and empty."

In the beginning God created the heavens and the earth. The earth was formless and void, and darkness was over the surface of the deep, and the Spirit of God was moving over the surface of the waters.

Genesis 1:1-2 NASB 1995

This formless and empty creation is portrayed as a mass of dark, chaotic waters. This first stage prepares us for the second, in which God, by his kingly authority, formed and filled his previously formless and empty creation. This was accomplished by his powerful Word and by the Spirit[2]. This second stage took place in an orderly way over a period of six days. He separated and gathered the elements he had created in order to give them form.[3] The sky, the seas and the dry ground thus appeared. He made new entities to fill the void.[4] He commanded these to produce something in order to fill the emptiness,[5] to order creation by separating and governing,[6] or to reproduce themselves and fill the place of their habitat.[7]

His forming involved the ordering and arranging of creation in such a way that it was fitted to be filled with the reflection of God himself. The entities with which he filled his creation reflect him in that they also form and/or fill and/or rule on a creaturely level.[8]

So why did God create in stages instead of creating everything in an instant? I believe one of the reasons was to reveal himself as a God of adventure. What is an adventure if not a mission that can be completed only by facing and overcoming obstacles and challenges? He created in stages to reveal himself as the God who faces and overcomes challenges. Of course, he is omnipotent. So, in that sense nothing is difficult for him. However, he wanted to show Adam and Eve—and their descendants—that he is the Great Adventurer.

This revelation of himself sets the stage for the mission he gave to mankind. The second stage of creation, in which God by his authoritative reign formed and filled what had been formless and empty, reached its climax on the sixth day with the creation of man. The text says:

> "Let Us make man in Our image, according to Our likeness; and let them rule over the fish of the sea and over the birds of the sky and over the cattle and over all the earth, and over every creeping thing that creeps on the earth." God created man in His own image, in the image of God He created him; male and female He created them.
> Genesis 1:26-27 NASB 1995

Man was set apart from the rest of creation because he was made in God's image. As the image of God, mankind was to imitate his Creator by ruling, forming and filling in a creaturely way the world that God had brought out of the chaotic waters. The human race was to take the creation which God had given them, the Garden and the undeveloped world that surrounded it, and—in imitation of God— bring it through a process of development as God had done in the second stage of creation. This can be seen in his command to Adam and Eve after creation.

> God blessed them; and God said to them, "Be fruitful and multiply, and fill the earth, and subdue it; and rule over the fish of the sea and over the birds of the sky and over every living thing that moves on the earth."
> Genesis 1:28 NASB 1995

In this verse they are commanded to:

1. Subdue the earth.
2. Be fruitful and increase in number.
3. Rule over the rest of creation.

Just as God formed and filled with his kingly authority, so Adam and Eve and their descendants are to imitate him by forming, filling and ruling.

The command to subdue the earth implies that after the second stage of creation, the world,[9] though "very good" and without defect, was still not in its final and fully developed state. In this way we see that God built adventure into his creation. This is evident from the meaning of the word "subdue." In the original Hebrew, the word subdue means "to make to serve, by force if necessary."[10] The writers of the *Theological Wordbook of the Old Testament* make this further comment:

> Therefore, "subdue" in Genesis 1:28 implies that creation will not do man's bidding gladly or easily and that man must now bring creation into submission by main strength. It is not to rule man.[11]

In other words, the pre-fall mission God gave to mankind was a challenging one—and a mission with a challenge is the very definition of adventure.

The command to subdue the earth reflects God's forming. Just as God brought order out of the chaotic waters by gathering and separating, so man must order the creation in such a way that its potential is developed, and it serves them as they serve God. They would begin the task in Eden and spread out to take the whole world.

The command to be fruitful, increase in number and fill the earth, echoes the command to the fish of the sea (verse 22). Adam and Eve are to have children and so to populate the whole earth with the human family. The implication is that man's task will be accomplished only with the combined effort of the entire human family covering the whole earth. The command to be fruitful certainly implies having children but may also include the fruitfulness of creating culture. In any case, the process of filling begun by God in the second stage of creation was to be carried on by mankind in a way consistent with being God's image. The stamp of God's character would be imprinted on his creation as his image filled the earth. This is so not only because man reflects God, but also because the relationship involved in being God's image implies that in some sense God is present with man.[12]

The third command—to rule—tells us explicitly that the human family is to be king over God's creation, with all the authority that such kingship implies. Mankind was to exercise kingship under God's kingship to make explicit and extend his kingly rule—his kingdom—over the whole earth.

This commission of Genesis 1:28, then, is made up of these three elements: kingly authority, forming control and filling presence. They reflect God's own authority, forming and filling as seen in the creation account.[13]

As God formed and filled what had been formless and empty, so man must use his God-given authority to order, arrange, subdue, control and fill the world with his presence. Mankind, of course, does not create out of nothing nor does he begin with unformed, unfilled being. Rather, he takes what God has created, formed and filled and —empowered by him— brings it to a more highly developed state. He imitates God's ruling, forming and filling on a creaturely level. In this way he must make explicit whatever implicit potentiality God placed within his creation.

The goal of this development was the rest of the seventh day.

> By the seventh day God completed His work which He had done, and He rested on the seventh day from all His work which He had done. Then God blessed the seventh day and sanctified it, because in it He rested from all His work which God had created and made.
>
> Genesis 2:1-3 NASB 1995

The seventh day shows us that God's original kingly forming and filling, as well as mankind's kingly forming and filling, had a goal in mind. The plan was never to stay in the Garden. It was always to make explicit God's rule over all the earth and to bring about a state of greater glory, anticipated in the Tree of Life, and here referred to as a sabbath rest. This rest is not to be understood as one of inactivity. Rather, it refers to the kind of rest, satisfaction and joy you get after having completed a challenging mission.[14]

The main point here is that when God created mankind in his image, giving us the task of utilizing delegated kingly authority to form and fill creation, he made us to be kingdom agents on an adventurous, challenging mission—even before the fall.

Pray as Agents on a Dangerous Mission

After the fall, of course, the human race became rebels. No one was able to represent God as his kingdom agent—that is, apart from his redemptive grace. In his grace, however, he chose men like Abraham, Moses and David to foreshadow[15] the coming of the final king—King Jesus—who on the basis of his death and resurrection is now the human king of the world. Through his death and resurrection, he initiated the final form of his kingdom—the promised Sabbath rest. Now—to a great extent through his people—he is advancing that kingdom. One day, at his second coming, he will bring the kingdom in its fullness.

In the meantime—as we await his second coming—the still challenging adventure takes on a new dimension for God's people: danger. It becomes a dangerous mission because now we must carry it out while facing an enemy who wants to keep us from doing so, and who wants to devour us like a lion devours its prey[16]. In addition, every person who has not been transferred by grace from the domain of darkness into the kingdom of Christ is his enemy.

In order for people to carry out their original mission as outlined in Genesis 1-2, God's enemies need to become his friends by accepting his (very excellent!) terms of surrender:[17] turn away from sin and believe in Christ and you will not only be forgiven but become a co-heir with Christ of all things[18]! Part of our dangerous mission is announcing God's terms of surrender to those who are still his enemies.[19] Although as believers we are citizens of the kingdom of Christ, our mission is carried out among those who are citizens of the domain of darkness. To carry out our mission, we must engage God's human enemies with his terms of surrender, and his demonic enemies with resistance[20].

Pray as Agents with Two Related Missions

Even after the fall, all people are under obligation to carry out the original mission given to us by God. Although even now unbelievers in some ways—and often unwittingly—carry out that original mission in spite of their rebellion, it's only believers in Christ who are able intentionally and with kingdom effectiveness to carry it out. For that reason—in order to restore people to their original mission—Christ gave his church what has come to be known as the Great Commission.

> And Jesus came up and spoke to them, saying, "All authority has been given to Me in heaven and on earth. Go therefore and make disciples of all the nations, baptizing them in the name of the Father and the Son and the Holy Spirit, teaching them to observe all that I commanded you; and lo, I am with you always, even to the end of the age."
> Matthew 28:18-20 NASB 1995

Jesus tells his disciples—and through them the church—to make disciples of all nations. People must enter the kingdom of God through repentance and faith before they can properly fulfill the original kingdom mission in Genesis. So, this Great Commission does not replace the original kingdom mission but makes it possible. Furthermore, this commission is not just for cross-cultural missionaries. Every Christian should be involved in it. Use your gifts in such a way that people become disciples and become more effective disciples.

Luke says in Acts 1:1 that his first book (Luke) was about "all that

Jesus *began* to do and to teach." This, of course, refers to his earthly ministry. The implication is that his second book—Acts—is about all that Jesus *continues* to do and to teach. However, this continuation of his ministry is quite different. In the next verses, just before he ascended into heaven, Jesus told his disciples to wait for the promised power of the Spirit to be his witnesses. In chapter 2 of Acts we read about the outpouring of the Spirit on all his people to give us power to carry on his ministry.

Jesus is no longer physically on earth but seated at the right hand of the Father. Now he continues his ministry through his Spirit-empowered people, protecting us from the enemy, reminding us of his finished work, praying for us, training us for greater effectiveness, and anchoring us to himself. Having empowered us by his Spirit, he now brings us into his adventure as key agents in the accomplishment of his mission. It is largely through us, his Spirit-filled people, that God brings out the full implications of his victory over sin, death and the evil one, and moves his kingdom toward its consummation.

Pray as Incognito Agents

Stories that have to do with concealed identity, in which the importance of the main character is not immediately visible, are fascinating to me. I'm talking about people who get things done by flying under the radar of societal expectations. Some examples that come to mind include spies, time travelers, and royalty whose identity must be temporarily hidden for their own protection (think Tolkien's Aragorn). For one reason or another, and in some way or another, these people all accomplish their goals by living incognito.

It shouldn't be surprising that this theme would be interesting since when God came to earth to live among us, he concealed his glory in interesting ways. Yes, he revealed it on specific occasions, especially to his disciples.[21] And one day he will return to reveal the fullness of his glory. But when the King of Kings came to earth, he was not born in a palace, he did not grow up in an important place, and he was not trained in the best schools of his day. In fact, when evaluated according to the societal expectations of his day,[22] he was a nobody.

Often when he revealed his glory through a miracle, he would command people not to tell others about it. Mark tells us why. It has to do with a prophecy of Isaiah:

> Many followed Him, and He healed them all, and warned them not to tell who He was. This was to fulfill what was spoken through Isaiah the prophet: "Behold, My Servant whom I have chosen; My Beloved in whom My soul is well-pleased; I will put My Spirit upon Him, And He shall proclaim justice to the Gentiles. "He will not quarrel, nor cry out; Nor will anyone hear His voice in the streets. "A battered reed He will not break off, And a smoldering wick He will not put out, Until He leads justice to victory. "And in His name the Gentiles will hope."
> Matthew 12:15-21 NASB 1995 quoting Isaiah 42:1-4

Jesus could easily have become famous according to the standards of fame in his day. But he wasn't looking for fame. His mission was to bring the justice of the kingdom of God to the earth. His mission was to replace the kingdoms of this world, infected by sin and its evil consequences, with that which is right and in harmony with the will of God. His methods did not include what was typically expected of the Messiah—stirring up crowds to overthrow the Romans. Rather, he was gentle with those who are weak and exhausted. As a result, one day his name would be proclaimed openly even among the Gentiles.

In fact, Jesus' goals could not be accomplished by becoming famous according to the standards of his day. While the society in which he lived was grasping after fame, he turned away from it. His brothers complained about this:

Therefore His brothers said to Him, "Leave here and go into Judea, so that Your disciples also may see Your works which You are doing. For no one does anything in secret when he himself seeks to be known publicly. If You do these things, show Yourself to the world." For not even His brothers were believing in Him.

John 7:3-5 NASB 1995

His insistence on the irrelevance of fame brought him into direct conflict with the leaders of his day, who were very interested in it. Jesus criticized them for it:

"When you pray, you are not to be like the hypocrites; for they love to stand and pray in the synagogues and on the street corners so that they may be seen by men. Truly I say to you, they have their reward in full.

Matthew 6:5 NASB 1995

It's certainly not wrong to pray in public. But the Pharisees did it to gain a reputation of being great and truly spiritual leaders. They were after the praise of men. Their mission was to establish their own kingdom. They wanted fame and glory not only for themselves, but also for the nation of Israel. They wanted to return to the glory they had under King David, with themselves in the honored places of leadership.

Jesus' confrontation of them and their beliefs, along with their envy of Jesus because of his popularity in spite of being a nobody and not caring about fame,[23] prompted them to crucify him. As it turns out though, this was part of God's plan all along.[24] He had sent the true Lamb of God[25] to suffer God's just wrath against those who have rejected God in favor of the praise of men. So, Jesus fulfilled his mission by living and ministering incognito.

Now that Jesus has conquered death, we are to proclaim his famous name openly. And one day this name will be known and honored among all peoples. In the meantime, those of us who are

Christ's disciples are called to follow his earthly example: to take up our cross and follow him, walking the way of the cross.[26]

This is part of the adventure. Carrying out our mission with our glory hidden in jars of clay is a clear challenge. Some Christians think that if we could just produce some famous Christians, the world would finally listen. Some ministers are also grasping after the recognition offered by society or by their denominational culture, maybe thinking that this fame and recognition are good for the progress of the kingdom. But the apostle Paul says,

> Therefore from now on we recognize no one according to the flesh; even though we have known Christ according to the flesh, yet now we know Him in this way no longer. Therefore if anyone is in Christ, he is a new creature; the old things passed away; behold, new things have come.
>
> 2 Corinthians 5:16-17 NASB 1995

"According to the flesh" means "according to what the world apart from Christ values." Paul says they once evaluated Christ and his ministry according to whether or not he was famous—well-regarded by society. But they learned to see in him the King bringing a whole new order in which these things didn't matter. What counts is not whether your appearance, gifts, abilities, knowledge and experience are valued by society. What counts is your participation in the new creation—the kingdom of God.[27] Whenever we use our gifts in a way designed to make ourselves look good, instead of making Christ look good, we are refusing to walk the incognito way of the cross.

While the Lord does, for his own reasons, sometimes permit some of his people to become famous according to the world, this is not what we should be looking for. It's not fame that makes us effective kingdom agents. It's not necessarily better for the progress of the kingdom to be famous. In fact, it can be very dangerous for believers to become famous. Fame easily goes to our head and renders us less effective kingdom agents. If the Lord should call you to it, may he give you the grace to bear it and resist the temptations that often come with fame.

No, he calls us to be more like undercover spies who, incognito and empowered by the Spirit of God, participate in the rescue of people from darkness and danger—more like the Scarlet Pimpernel[28] or the Lone Ranger than Beowulf or King Arthur. He calls us to be more like time travelers from the future who know the glory they will one day have, but who for now keep a low profile. Since the future eschatological kingdom has entered into our world beforehand, in the midst of weakness, sin and death, we announce the presence and power of the future glory that will someday be fully revealed. We pray for the full coming of the kingdom. But we do so "in secret."

> But you, when you pray, go into your inner room, close your door
> and pray to your Father who is in secret, and your Father who sees
> what is done in secret will reward you.
> Matthew 6:6 NASB 1995

The point is not to avoid public prayer. The point is to avoid praying in a way designed to bring attention to yourself. We are praying for the coming of the kingdom, not as a way to be recognized or bring glory to ourselves.

He calls us, who are destined to be heirs of the whole world,[29] to accept our glorious inheritance by faith and to be willing to walk incognito in order to carry out our mission. Indeed, there is a sense in which we are secret agents on an adventurous mission. In this time between the initiation of the kingdom and its fullness, we are to pray as secret kingdom agents who are not concerned about their own glory but the full coming of the glorious kingdom of Christ.

Rest for the Adventurer

Sometimes people get excited about being on an adventure. At other times they are overwhelmed by adventures that seem too challenging. The Lord provides rest as well as adventure. At the very beginning— even before the fall—he told us that he himself rested from his work. In other words, he accomplished his mission of creation, sat on his throne and rejoiced in his accomplishment. Someday believers in Christ will finally enter that rest—we will have completed our assigned mission.[30] In the meantime, Jesus has won the victory over the evil one and as the Second Adam has already fully entered into that rest. He tells us to come to him and rest. He says,

> Come to Me, all who are weary and heavy-laden, and I will give you rest. Take My yoke upon you and learn from Me, for I am gentle and humble in heart, and you will find rest for your souls. For My yoke is easy and My burden is light.
> Matthew 11:28-30 NASB 1995

One of the main ways we come to him for rest is through prayer. When we pray as an adventurer, we also come to him in prayer seeking needed rest along the way.

Adventure and the Church Today

I believe the church today in the United States has for the most part lost this Biblical sense of adventure. It has lost its willingness to face challenges in the name of kingdom advance. Imagine an 18-year-old who was over-protected by his parents. He didn't have the opportunity to discover the kinds of things he was capable of because his parents protected him from facing challenges. Let's imagine they did this in the name of love. They wanted to protect him because they cared about him. It was only many years later, when they saw his fear of facing challenges and his unhealthy dependence on them that they realized their error—and the wonderful benefits of facing challenges.

In a similar way the church has over-protected believers. Because of the beneficial influence of the gospel in our culture, we have experienced wonderful foretastes of the eschatological glory to come. In spite of our current economic woes, we are probably still the wealthiest culture in history. Through technology and other scientific discoveries, we have been able to overcome many effects of the fall.

But these wonderful foretastes seem to have dulled our Biblical sense of adventure. We have become so accustomed to money and technology eliminating challenges that we have lost sight of the Biblical challenges before us. And in many ways the church and its leadership have affirmed this mentality. We have become so enamored with the experience of a *foretaste* of glory that we barely yearn for the eschatological glory to come. Furthermore, having our desire for eschatological glory dulled, we are no longer willing to suffer the challenges involved in Biblical adventure, which has been relegated to the work of cross-cultural missionaries. I don't mean all such missionaries—just the ones who work in primitive conditions. These are considered to be the true adventurers of the church. But God calls all his people to engage in this adventure.

Being a kingdom agent doesn't necessarily mean selling everything you have and going overseas to be a foreign missionary. For *most* people it doesn't mean that. And going overseas doesn't make you a better kingdom agent than those who stay in their own culture. Being an effective kingdom agent doesn't necessarily mean becoming famous in your culture. The Lord's grace is effective in us as we are willing to be weak and unrecognized. Being an effective kingdom agent doesn't necessarily mean doing some great thing. The Lord works through us as we carry out simple acts of kindness, like giving a cup of cold water in his name.

Being a kingdom agent means making disciples as you go about ruling over, forming and filling the earth—in whatever areas God has gifted you and wherever on earth he has placed you. Making disciples requires not only communicating truth with your words but incarnating the truth in whatever ways and places God has called you to rule over, form and fill the earth. It requires getting to know and interacting with the people the Lord has in his providence placed in your path. There should be no dichotomy in our minds between being a kingdom agent and doing the jobs the Lord has called us to do. It's in the midst of the latter that you can effectively do the former. If you are a believer in Christ, you have been called as an agent of the kingdom to the greatest adventure of all time.

Follow-up

1. Have you ever thought that foreign missionaries are the true adventurers in the church? If so, give an example,

2. How do you feel now about having been chosen by God to be an adventurer in an important mission?

3. How do you typically face the challenges the Lord gives you?

4. Where do you typically get the strength to face the challenges in your life? What needs to happen to help you feel strong?

5. Do you think the church has lost its sense of adventure? Give your reasons for your answer.

6. Have you lost your sense of Biblical adventure? Explain with examples.

7. What do you think and how do you feel about the assertion that God typically uses people who aren't famous to advance his kingdom purposes?

8. How do you feel about being a secret agent for the kingdom of God?

Chapter 4

Pray as a Warrior

W e arrived in Chile as missionaries in the early 1980's. As I look back now, I realize that some of the differences that at first I perceived as cultural were actually a result of the fact that Chile never experienced the kind of strong impact of the gospel that the United States did in its early years. The Reformation had not arrived in Chile as it had in my own country.[1] As a result, the forces of evil were not as restricted in Chile. Toward the end of the 1980's, my wife and I read Frank Peretti's books *This Present Darkness*[2] and *Piercing the Darkness*.[3] Even though I may not agree with all his ideas on the spiritual battle in which we are engaged, it was a very good reminder of its reality.

As citizens of the kingdom, we are at war. Praying for the full coming of the kingdom means involvement in warfare against the defeated but still roaring and dangerous forces of evil that are determined to undermine the kingdom of God. The holy wars in the Old Testament are fulfilled in Christ. He himself suffered the bloody curse of death—eternal death— deserved by all humanity. During the Now-But-Not-Yet kingdom he offers terms of peace to all who will surrender to him. During this time our warfare is spiritual. The war in which we are engaged is a war over the eternal destiny of mankind. Those who belong to him will respond in faith. Those who do not will suffer the eternal curse at Jesus' second coming when he will judge the world.

I sometimes wonder how our prayer life would change if we were able to actually see the spiritual war between the angels and the demons going on around us as they battle for the allegiance of humanity--like when God opened the eyes of Elisha's servant to see God's army protecting them from the enemy.[4] But the Bible asks us to "see" it by faith. An ancient Greek hymn tries to help us take seriously this unseen reality when it says,

"Christian, dost thou see them on the holy ground, how the powers of darkness rage thy steps around?"[5]

Are you involved in the war that is raging around you? Could a listener tell by hearing you pray?

The Enemy

The church has an enemy who hates us because he hates Christ. The apostle Paul warns us about him:

Finally, be strong in the Lord and in the strength of His might. Put on the full armor of God, so that you will be able to stand firm against the schemes of the devil. For our struggle is not against flesh and blood, but against the rulers, against the powers, against the world forces of this darkness, against the spiritual forces of wickedness in the heavenly places.
Ephesians 6:10-12 NASB 1995

This enemy would love to eat us up—that is, increase his area of selfhood at our expense.[6] Our enemy is on the offensive and determined to bring us to hell and/or make us ineffective in battle. He doesn't want us to be like Christ. He wants us to be captivated by our society with its system of rewards and punishments. He wants us to give in to the tug of the flesh. As Martin Luther said, he is "armed with cruel hate."[7]

He has a powerful, large and well-organized army. They are not mere flesh and blood. In God's permissive providence, they are in control of the world of sin. They are the rulers, authorities and powers of this dark world.[8] As Martin Luther said, "On earth is not his equal."[9]

The enemy is crafty. As Martin Luther said, "His craft and power are great."[10] Here are some of his crafty ways:[11]

1. He mixes error with truth so as to make it sound plausible.[12]
2. He quotes Scripture out of context for his own evil purposes.[13]
3. He masquerades as an angel of light[14]
4. He suggests that good can be accomplished through wrongdoing.[15]
5. He lies.[16]
6. He tries to discourage God's people so that, overcome with anxiety and fear, they falter or stop acting on the basis of the truth of God's Word.[17]
7. He tries to incapacitate God's people by making success go to their heads.[18]

We should remember that the devil is a defeated foe and cannot stand up against the power of God.[19] By God's grace that power is available to God's people and we, by grace through faith, can stand up against him. As Martin Luther said, "One little word shall fell him." However, this will happen only if we fight.

The Fight

We are called to fight as significant kingdom agents. Hendriksen puts the issue in perspective:

> Not only this or that particular battle but the entire war will be lost unless we exert ourselves. It is true that the counsel of God from eternity will never fail, but it is just as true that in that plan of God from eternity it was decided that victory will be given to those who overcome (Rev. 2:7, 11, 17, etc.). Over-comers are conquerors, and in order to conquer one must fight![20]

One of the most dangerous things for the believer is to be lulled to sleep in the midst of this spiritual battle—to give in to the status quo of the point system[21] of our society. He who sleeps is sure to suffer the consequences, including setbacks for the advancement of the kingdom.

The battle is constant. However, Paul warns us to be prepared for the "evil day" in which the battle will be particularly fierce.

> Therefore, take up the full armor of God, so that you will be able to resist in the evil day, and having done everything, to stand firm.
>   Ephesians 6:13 NASB 1995

Since we never know when these especially fierce attacks may come, we must always be engaged in offensive warfare and always be ready for defensive maneuvers.

The Armor

God's people should make prayer a priority as we engage in the spiritual warfare to which we have been called. In Ephesians 6:14-20 Paul explains in detail the importance of using God's armor as we engage in warfare. Our seven weapons include the belt of truth, the breastplate of righteousness, shoes that because of the gospel are ready for action, the shield of faith, the helmet of salvation, the sword of the Spirit, and prayer, which is "the climax of them all."[22] After listing the other six weapons, Paul says,

> With all prayer and petition pray at all times in the Spirit, and with this in view, be on the alert with all perseverance and petition for all the saints....
>   Ephesians 6:18 NASB 1995

In this passage about Christian warfare Paul alludes to Isaiah 59:16-17 in which God, having been astonished that there was no one to intercede in prayer for his wayward people, takes actions himself to rescue them. He himself puts on righteousness as body armor and a helmet of salvation in order to rescue his people from their sin. This he has done in Christ. He has won the victory. Those of us who are in Christ now have the privilege of putting on this same armor of God. We are his kingdom agents through whom he brings out all the implications of his victory over the enemy. One of the ways we do this is through prayer.

In other words, prayer is part of the required armor. We must not take it lightly. According to Paul, as we put on and use the armor of God for warfare, we are to be praying (1) on all occasions, (2) with all kinds of prayers and requests, (3) in the Spirit, (4) with alert perseverance, and (5) for all the saints.

On All Occasions

There is a tendency to confine prayer to (1) times of special need, and (2) certain designated times like prayer meetings. I have noticed that many churches in my own culture spend very little time praying together. I have also noticed that in many prayer meetings so much time is spent talking about prayer requests—or talking about other things—that very little time is left afterwards for actual prayer. This kind of limited communication would be disastrous in physical warfare. And so it is in kingdom warfare.

I don't think this talking time is unimportant. Care must be taken that it doesn't lead to gossip or self-centered expressions. But I do think it is important for God's people to clarify to themselves just what they should be praying about. Talking about the different challenges they face and bringing God's Word to bear so the situation can be properly framed is important to prayer. This is one of the things "on all occasions" implies. We should pray about every situation that faces us and clarify just what that situation is.

I suggest that when ministry groups pray together, they should normally focus on the mission before them and the issues that impinge on that mission. More personal prayer requests that are not as relevant to the mission of the group can normally be prayed for in other settings. On the other hand, personal issues can impinge on the group. So, I don't think it's wrong to include personal prayer requests. It's a matter of emphasis. If the personal requests push out the ministry prayer, then to that extent they are out of place.

Praying on all occasions also implies praying more freely throughout the day, and not restricting prayer to special designated prayer times. Other verses also encourage us along these lines:

> Pray without ceasing.
> 1 Thessalonians 5:17 NASB 1995
> Devote yourselves to prayer.
> Colossians 4:2 NASB 1995
> Is anyone among you suffering? Then he must pray. Is anyone cheerful? He is to sing praises.
> James 5:13 NASB 1995

While I'm sure I don't measure up to the Biblical ideal, and I still feel the tug of the flesh not to pray, over the years I have increasingly found myself praying throughout the day and in various venues. For example, I'm talking to someone about a situation. We seem to have clarified what the situation is. Then we pray about it then and there. Or sometimes the Lord seems to bring someone to my mind--either through some circumstance that reminds me of them, or even through a dream. In Philippians 1:3 Paul says, "I thank my God every time I remember you." What I'm saying is that I've learned to pay more attention to those things the Lord brings to my mind,[23] and to take them as a prompting and opportunity to pray.

All Kinds of Prayers and Requests

If you listen to a group of people talking, normally you will hear all kinds of expressions: statements, questions, exclamations; requests, demands, words of thanks; admiration, gratitude, and so on. Human speech can be quite varied. Sometimes, though, you come across someone who seems to have only one way of communicating. Some people, for example, talk almost exclusively about themselves. Others are always trying to get you to do something for them or trying to control you. Most people do not enjoy communication that is thus reduced.

When we talk to God in prayer, our speech should be as varied as our experience. Most prayer meetings I've attended focus on requests. Additionally, they focus on a certain kind of request: those related to me and mine. While it is certainly proper and good to pray for self, family and friends, Paul says we should make "all kinds of prayers and requests." This includes, of course, things like confession of sin, praise and worship of God, thankfulness, and requests for more than me and mine. In other words, the kinds of prayers we are to make run the gamut of human experience. So "all kinds of prayers" corresponds to "on all occasions." Pray not only when you need something but also when you are thankful, for example. Because we are praying for the full coming of the kingdom, and since everything relates to the kingdom, we should pray all kinds of prayers. Effective warfare requires it.

In the Spirit

Waging effective spiritual war requires praying in the Spirit. William Hendriksen interprets praying "in the Spirit" to mean "with his help" and "in harmony with his will" as revealed in the Word which he inspired.[24] I will share some of my thoughts on both of these and add a third.

In Harmony with His Will

When we look at God's will as applied to requests, for example, we should pray in the context of:

1. What God has promised.
2. God's commands.
3. God's attributes and character.
4. God's mighty works.
5. How all these are fulfilled in Christ.
6. Application to the church which is united to Christ.

In practice, this usually works itself out in giving God Biblical reasons why he should answer our prayers.[25] Here are a few examples of what this might look like. We ask because:

1. You promised.
2. You commanded.
3. You are holy, or sovereign, or compassionate, etc.
4. You rescued your people from the hand of Pharaoh, etc.
5. You sent Jesus to defeat death and sin, etc.
6. We are your people for whom Christ died. You have seated us in the heavenly realms. Etc.

It's a good practice to ask yourself why you are requesting whatever you are requesting. Sometimes people haven't thought through the reasons for their request. To the extent that people are captivated by the circumstantial perspective, the reason for their requests will be to have good circumstances and avoid bad ones. Developing the habit of giving Biblical reasons will help us pray in harmony with his will.

With His Help

We are weak when it comes to knowing what to pray for. However, thanks to God that

> In the same way the Spirit also helps our weakness; for we do not know how to pray as we should, but the Spirit Himself intercedes for us with groanings too deep for words; and He who searches the hearts knows what the mind of the Spirit is, because He intercedes for the saints according to the will of God.
>
> Romans 8:26-27 NASB 1995

Giving Biblical reasons could easily become a mere technique. The point is to understand God's heart about the challenges and opportunities we face in ministry. But our faith in Christ is in process. It is not fully grown. Our vision is not fully clear as we pray for God's will in a particular situation. We don't always know what to pray for, or how best to formulate the prayer.

For this reason, the Spirit helps us. As Christ intercedes for us in heaven, so the Spirit intercedes for us within us. As he intercedes, he groans because he longs to see our faith fully developed and to see us more capable of understanding just how to pray in accordance with God's will. And he also has compassion on us in our weakness. He looks at the seed of faith within us at whatever stage of development, and for the sake of Christ who died for us, he intercedes in a much clearer way than we are able to pray. And his intercession is fully in accord with God's will. For this reason, it is always effective.

The Spirit helps us as we look to Christ in faith at whatever level of growth we happen to find ourselves. In other words, the Spirit takes our prayers offered with imperfect faith, and edits them in a way that expresses perfectly what is to some extent only implicit in our faith. His edits are fully in line with God's will. Sincere faith in

Christ, whether from a new convert or a more mature child of God, is enough grounds for the Spirit to intercede on our behalf.

When I was planting a church in Chile, I noticed that new converts were very hesitant to pray. When I asked them about it, they would say, "I don't know how." Upon further investigation, I discovered that those of us who had more experience in the Lord's kingdom were unintentionally communicating that there is a certain formula that has to be followed in prayer. I discovered that certain phrases like "if it be thy will," and "we beg you," and saying the word "Lord" every few words did not fit with the way people talked with each other. It seemed to new converts like a specialized way of talking that they had not mastered. Of course, there are things we need to learn about prayer. But on one level it's just talking to God. And if we don't do it perfectly, the Spirit is there to intercede for us. So don't wait until you've mastered some socially accepted technique before you begin to pray and give Biblical reasons for your prayers. The Spirit intercedes on our behalf and thus helps us in our weakness.

With his Power

Believers in Christ do not have the power in themselves to bring forward God's kingdom purposes. But as we respond in faith to who God is, what he has done, and what he promises to do in Christ, the Spirit flows out from us with power akin to that of many life-giving rivers. It's this supernatural power that enables us to accomplish— through our prayers and actions—what would otherwise be impossible for us. Listen to Jesus' words:

> Now on the last day, the great day of the feast, Jesus stood and cried out, saying, "If anyone is thirsty, let him come to Me and drink. 38 He who believes in Me, as the Scripture said, 'From his innermost being will flow rivers of living water.'" But this He spoke of the Spirit, whom those who believed in Him were to receive; for the Spirit was not yet given, because Jesus was not yet glorified.
> John 7:37-39 NASB 1995

Jesus here equates drinking of him with having faith in him. Having faith in Jesus cannot be reduced to that first moment someone believes and becomes a follower of Christ. Rather, it means putting your faith to work in every situation. For example, every time we worry, what we are saying, in effect, is something like this, "Jesus, thank you that you died for me and conquered death, but that's not enough. Fix this situation that I'm worrying about for me—make it go away—and then I'll be able to serve you." Every time we are consumed with anger, we are saying, "Jesus, thank you for dying for me, but it's not enough. Get that person to say he's sorry for offending me, and then I'll be able to forgive him." Every time we're motivated by envy, we're saying, "Jesus, thank you that you died for me, but it's not enough. If I could only have this one thing, I would be happy to serve you." Every time we are filled with self-pity, what we are saying for all practical purposes is this; "Jesus, thank you that you died for me, but it's not enough. Help me to feel better about myself, and then I'll be able to serve you." Praying in faith means putting your faith to work in every situation, while resisting the temptation to be sucked into and controlled by the values (point system) of the surrounding culture. In all these examples, something has for all practical purposes become more important than Christ. These situations call for repentance and renewed faith.

The rivers of living water are the Holy Spirit who would be poured out on the day of Pentecost. All it takes is one sip of Jesus—one look away from ourselves and to him in faith—for the power of the Spirit to flow out from us like rivers of life to accomplish God's kingdom purposes. When we are empty and grasping for something to fill us up and make us feel good about ourselves, our prayers are not effective. Believers should not be empty and grasping for something to give meaning to our lives. Rather, we should be full of the Spirit and overflowing with rivers of life. Our prayers are Spirit-empowered and are effective in warfare to bring about the fullness of God's kingdom as we pray in faith.

With Alert Perseverance

There is a sense in which Christian growth is a process of becoming aware: of your sin, of the power and evil of the enemy, of what God has done and is doing in Christ, and the nature of your particular role in the kingdom. The flesh tempts us to fall asleep instead of pressing on in faith to greater levels of awareness. The culture in which we live tempts us to focus our eyes and hearts on anything other than Christ. The evil one wants to get us off track and devour us. There is pressure from every side to become less vigilant, to get off-track, or to give up. In moments of crisis, we tend to become more alert. But the Lord wants all our prayers to be characterized by an intentional effort to be aware of what is going on, in our hearts, in his Word, in our neighborhood, church and world.

This requires self-discipline. Paul tells Timothy, "Train yourself for godly living."[26] This does not imply salvation by works. Rather, we are to put our faith to work. The word "train" in this verse comes from the world of the Greek gymnasium. Just as people exercise to get their bodies in shape, so we should put our faith to work. Don't sit back and wait for God to somehow transform you into a godly person. As you contemplate what God has done for you in Christ, apply it to such simple things as eating well and getting a good night's sleep.[27] Schedule time to read the Bible and pray. Let those be some of the immovable rocks around which the stream of life flows instead of including them only when other priorities permit.

For All the Saints

Obviously, no one but Christ can pray for every saint individually. But we can and should pray in general for all the saints. We should pray for those who are being persecuted for the sake of the kingdom, even though we may not know who they are specifically. We should pray for all different kinds of saints, and not just for "me and mine." We should pray for Christian leaders and followers, for the wealthy and the poor, for the famous and the unknown, for the sick and the healthy. We should pray more specifically for those saints the Lord has placed in our path. In the book of Ephesians there is an emphasis on the unity of the saints. We need each other, so it is in our best interest to pray for each other. It may be the person at church who rubs you the wrong way that you need most in order to grow. So, pray for that person!

Conclusion

During my first church plant, I challenged some young men to allow me to train them for ministry. One of the things we did was to pray together every morning for about two hours. I tried to teach them how to pray in the way I'm describing. That was over 30 years ago, and since then I think I've learned more about it. But we did our best at the level of faith we had at that time to pray kingdom prayers that would be useful in battle. And the Lord blessed our efforts. During the next 8 months as we prayed, we saw more people—about sixty—come to know the Lord and join the church than we had ever seen before.

I would like to challenge ministry groups of all kinds to take at least five hours a week to do warfare through prayer in which situations are clarified through dialogue and by bringing God's Word to bear in the context of faith in Christ. The more you are involved in the battle by using your gifts in faith to reach out to others, the more you will need to pray. This is an extremely important part of church planting and ministry in general. If five hours a week seems like too much, start with what you can manage and see where it leads you.

I suggest clarifying and praying for one issue at a time instead of clarifying all issues first and then praying for all of them. I suggest this because it seems to help the group not get so involved in "clarifying" that in the end they don't have time to pray. But each group should find the way that works best for them. We are at war! The Lord uses our prayers to bring about the victory of his kingdom.

* * *

Follow-up

1. Does it seem to you that you are in a life and death battle? Give your evidence or reasons.
2. Examine your prayers. Notice to what extent you pray "all kinds of prayers." If you find yourself over focused on requests or some other area, why do you think that is? Make an effort to pray "all kinds of prayers."
3. As you continue to examine your prayers, to what extent do you give Biblical reasons for your prayers? If you don't do this very much, why do you think that is? Make an effort to relate your prayers to Biblical reasons and realities.
4. Listen to the prayers of your church prayer meetings. To what extent do the people in these meetings pray "all kinds of prayers," and give Biblical reasons to accompany them?
5. When you pray in public, how concerned are you about praying in a way that will be acceptable to that group? If you find yourself concerned about this, why do you think that is? What do you think you should do about it? As you pray, remember that the Spirit helps you in your weakness. You don't have to be a super Christian with all the right words to make warfare through prayer.
6. What do you think about the fact that every time you are anxious, wrongfully angry, envious, proud, or full of self-pity you are actually to that extent rejecting Christ and not acting in faith? In this atmosphere of unbelief, our prayers are hindered. If necessary, take time to repent of being empty and grasping instead of full and overflowing with the Spirit.

7. Do you feel a need for greater discipline in the war in which you find yourself? Describe the details of that need. Remember the pertinent truths from God's Word and act in faith on the basis of those truths, and not on the basis of any feelings that are keeping you from prayer. Schedule time for doing warfare through prayer. If you find yourself too sleepy, discipline yourself to get into a regular sleeping pattern that gives you enough sleep. Maybe you are filling your time with things that aren't that important. Decide what things you can let go. Make prayer one of the rocks in your life around which other things flow.

8. For whom do you pray? Make a list of the people you regularly pray for. How varied is that list? If it helps you to pray for "all the saints," make a list of people to pray for and decide how often you will pray for them. You might pray for some people every day, and others weekly or every two weeks.

Chapter 5

Pray with Audacity

Audacity is shameless daring. It's something that doesn't come naturally to me. Even though I've had to raise funds as a missionary, it's not something I enjoy doing. My approach has basically been, "Here's what the Lord is doing and here is the need." I could never enjoy being a professional fund raiser who says, "I want you to consider generously giving ten million dollars toward this cause."

In the Now-But-Not-Yet kingdom, however, we are not to be asking politely for small adjustments in our lives and in world affairs but shamelessly for the transformation of the world—organized as it is against Christ—into the fullness of his glorious kingdom. We are called to be audacious in our kingdom agency.

The Subduing Effect of the World

The New Testament often uses the word "world" to indicate society as organized against Christ and his kingdom. Here are some examples:

Do not love the world nor the things in the world. If anyone loves the world, the love of the Father is not in him. For all that is in the world, the lust of the flesh and the lust of the eyes and the boastful pride of life, is not from the Father, but is from the world. The world is passing away, and also its lusts; but the one who does the will of God lives forever.

1 John 2:15-17 NASB 1995

Therefore I urge you, brethren, by the mercies of God, to present your bodies a living and holy sacrifice, acceptable to God, which is your spiritual service of worship.

Romans 12:1 NASB 1995

See to it that no one takes you captive through philosophy and empty deception, according to the tradition of men, according to the elementary principles of the world, rather than according to Christ.

Colossians 2:8 NASB 1995

The various cultures or societies in which we live are structured in ways designed to subdue the audacity of God's people. This "world" attempts to seduce us to love it and pressures us to conform the way we think and live to its perspective. It does this so it can captivate us and render us ineffective as kingdom agents.

So just what is this worldly perspective? I like to describe it as a societal point system that is used to measure the worth of people. While I will discuss this topic in more depth in the following chapter, I want to touch on it here. The system of points in a given culture is not usually explicit, but members of any given society know intuitively what it is. The point system says, "You are valuable if you have certain possessions, characteristics or abilities." Again, the exact number of points assigned to something is not explicit, but members of the society know intuitively how much something is worth relative to other things. Here are some of the things a society might value:

1. Being wealthy

2. Being handsome or pretty
3. Being intelligent
4. Having a winsome personality
5. Having some outstanding ability
6. Having a doctorate
7. Owning your own home
8. Being a "go-getter"
9. Having a nice car
10. Being the president of some important organization

The specific ways these points are assigned may differ from one culture to another. For example, in Latin America having a winsome personality is valued more than it is in the culture of the United States. Being a "go-getter" is valued more in the US than in Latin America. So, what is valued—and how much it is valued—may differ from culture to culture. But all societies are similar in that they all have winners and losers. The winners are those who have the most societal points, while the losers are those who have the least.

Within any given society, the various subcultures within it are likely to have variations of the societal point system. Churches, to the extent they are influenced by this system, develop their own version. Here are some of the typical components of such a point system:

1. Being a long-standing member of the church
2. Being a leader in the church
3. Being the pastor of the church
4. Knowing more theology than others
5. Being a pastor who is often invited to speak at other events
6. Being the pastor of a large church
7. Being a missionary who is apparently willing to give up the points he could have had by staying home

The apostle Paul refers to this point system when he says,

Therefore from now on we recognize no one according to the flesh; even though we have known Christ according to the flesh, yet now we know Him in this way no longer. Therefore if anyone is in Christ, he is a new creature; the old things passed away; behold, new things have come.

   2 Corinthians 5:16-17 NASB 1995

To regard people according to the flesh is to regard them apart from Christ—that is, according to their societal point system.[1] We can get a glimpse of the societal point system of the culture in which Jesus was born and ministered. One of the most important values was the nation returning to the glory and power they had under David and Solomon. During the time of Jesus, they were no longer "the head" of the nations, but "the tail," under the control of the Roman Empire. Because of this value, the disciples often misunderstood Jesus' words and actions. For example, Peter rebuked him when he spoke of the need to die. The disciples didn't want Jesus to die. They wanted him to overthrow the Romans and exalt Israel among the nations. They wanted to have the places of honor in that new kingdom. As discussed in chapter one, they were caught up in the circumstantial perspective, which means they were to some extent captivated by their societal point system. As a result, they said and did foolish things, and didn't know how to pray. Their prayers were circumscribed and subdued by the values of their societal point system.

Asking for the Outrageously Impossible

In the Now-But-Not-Yet kingdom, our actions and prayers are not to be limited by the values of our societal point system. When Jesus withered the fig tree he said,

And Jesus answered and said to them, "Truly I say to you, if you have faith and do not doubt, you will not only do what was done to the fig tree, but even if you say to this mountain, 'Be taken up and cast into the sea,' it will happen. And all things you ask in prayer, believing, you will receive."

Matthew 21:21-22 NASB 1995

The Old Testament connects the removal of mountains with the coming of God's kingdom rule.[2]

A voice is calling, "Clear the way for the Lord in the wilderness; Make smooth in the desert a highway for our God. "Let every valley be lifted up, And every mountain and hill be made low; And let the rough ground become a plain, And the rugged terrain a broad valley;"

Isaiah 40:3-4[3] NASB 1995

We should ask—in specific ways—that the full implications of Jesus' victory over death and hell be manifest in our day and in the situations we face. We should ask that the kingdoms of this world be fully replaced by the kingdom of our Lord. We should ask for radical change everywhere. We should ask that Jesus everywhere be acknowledged as king. We should ask to be filled with the most powerful force in the universe—the Holy Spirit—so we can accomplish the impossible. That is audacious prayer.

Jesus asked his listeners to imagine themselves in need of bread late at night. You hate to wake anyone at this time of night, but your need is great. So, you go to a friend at midnight to ask for three loaves of bread. Jesus says,

I tell you, even though he will not get up and give him anything because he is his friend, yet because of his persistence he will get up and give him as much as he needs. "So I say to you, ask, and it will be given to you; seek, and you will find; knock, and it will be opened to you.

Luke 11:8-9 NASB 1995

Waking someone at midnight is audacious. Society would say, "How dare they make such a request! It's just not right!" So it is that many people approach God in prayer—as if they didn't want to offend him by asking for anything too great. We don't want to be a bother. Just a little blessing here, and tweak there in society—nothing too difficult, nothing outrageous. Just make me comfortable. Just give me societal points. Help our church to grow so outsiders will see how important we are and come join us. Make us famous so we can have greater kingdom impact. Maybe deep down we don't really expect God to do much, so we only ask for things that don't seem too difficult. Do we think he's more likely to answer if it's not such an audacious request? Quite the opposite is true!

The apostle Paul encourages us to pray audacious prayers by indicating just how much God is willing and able to do for his children. He says that God

...is able to do far more abundantly than all that we ask or imagine.
Ephesians 3:20[4]

Listen to Hendrickson's comments on this verse:

"In order to appreciate fully what is implied in these words it should be noted that Paul's reasoning has taken the following steps: a. God is able to do all we ask him to do; b. he is even able to do all that we dare not ask but merely imagine; c. he can do more than this; d. far more; e. very far more."[5]

The coming of the kingdom doesn't happen through tweaks. In fact, the things we need to ask in order for the kingdom to come are not even merely difficult. There is a sense in which when we pray we are audaciously asking for the impossible.

My first assignment as a church planter in Chile was to grow and organize a church on the poorer side of town. I was the only person in the church who owned a car. So, I often found myself bringing our church people to the emergency room when they needed emergency medical attention. I discovered that there were two kinds of medical insurance in the country: one for the wealthy that was just as good as any I'd ever seen, and one for the poor that was not good at all. I found that in most cases the doctor would just give them a pain shot and send them home. Several of us became increasingly upset at the social injustice. The members of our church were prevented from getting medical attention. The kingdom had come, but they were being marginalized. Society was organized against them. Something needed to be done. The Lord directed my thoughts to James' comments on praying for the sick:

> Is anyone among you sick? Then he must call for the elders of the church and they are to pray over him, anointing him with oil in the name of the Lord; and the prayer offered in faith will restore the one who is sick, and the Lord will raise him up, and if he has committed sins, they will be forgiven him. Therefore, confess your sins to one another, and pray for one another so that you may be healed. The effective prayer of a righteous man can accomplish much.
>   James 5:14-16 NASB 1995

My first reaction was to keep looking for some other solution. Although I certainly believed that God could heal the sick if he wanted to, I belong to a tradition that tends not to put this passage on its list of favorites. I was torn. On the one hand, there was the passage staring me right in the face. Every time I looked it said the same thing. On the other hand, it seemed a little too audacious to take it at face value. Is this really going to be the solution to our existential problem? Eventually we couldn't resist the force of the passage. So, we began praying for the sick during the worship service every Sunday. I had the ruling elders come up front with me and we prayed for those who came forward, anointing them with oil.

Several weeks later I wondered if the Lord was healing people in response to our prayers. I investigated. Again and again, people would tell me, "Of course, pastor. The Lord healed me." Not everyone said this. Not everyone was healed. But it was amazing to me how many people were. This encouraged my faith and gave me confidence to keep going. One time a leader from my mission agency was visiting. He went forward for prayer that Sunday. Later he told me he had felt an unusual and troubling pain in his heart and that the Lord healed him when the elders prayed for him. On another occasion we saw the Lord restore to health someone the doctors said was going to die shortly.

It's not necessarily wrong to ask for good circumstances, for comfort, for health. But when these are disconnected from the kingdom, they are not audacious prayers. Ask for the outrageously impossible. Ask for the kingdom in specific ways that connect with your situation.

Asking the Father

One of the reasons Christians might shy away from audacious prayers could be a sense of inadequacy. Someone might think, "I'm no great saint. Who am I to ask for such things?" But God's people should have shameless audacity in prayer because, for the sake of Christ who reconciled us to God, we can approach him and call him "Father." The relationship between father and child is intimate. A child can go to his or her father and ask for anything. Listen to the words of Jesus:

> Now suppose one of you fathers is asked by his son for a fish; he will not give him a snake instead of a fish, will he? Or if he is asked for an egg, he will not give him a scorpion, will he? If you then, being evil, know how to give good gifts to your children, how much more will your heavenly Father give the Holy Spirit to those who ask Him?"
>
> Luke 11:11-13 NASB 1995

If someone asks his earthly father for food, the father will not give him a stone or a snake. *How much more* will the heavenly Father give what is good to those who ask. If we fail to ask the Heavenly Father for what we need and desire in line with his kingdom promises—even impossibly outrageous things—we are in effect saying that God isn't even as good as our earthly fathers.

The author of Hebrews tells us that, in light of Jesus' once-for-all death and resurrection, we can now enter into the Holy of Holies—into the very presence of the Father.

> Therefore, brethren, since we have confidence to enter the holy place by the blood of Jesus, by a new and living way which He inaugurated for us through the veil, that is, His flesh, and since we have a great priest over the house of God, let us draw near with a sincere heart in full assurance of faith, having our hearts sprinkled clean from an evil conscience and our bodies washed with pure water.
>
> Hebrews 10:19-22 NASB 1995

Having this privilege would have been unthinkable to Old Testament saints. Only the high priest could enter, and only once a year. Now, however, we can have the audacity to enter into the presence of the Father and make requests of him.

We should pray with shameless audacity because we have a Heavenly Father who is more than willing to hear us. He would bend over backwards—in fact he sent his Son to die—to give us his Holy Spirit and get us engaged in his kingdom plan as significant kingdom agents to accomplish the impossible.

Doing the Impossible

Many television shows and movies have moments in which the situation looks clearly impossible. The hero has gotten himself or herself into a jam, and it looks like there's no way out. Sometimes at those moments I say to my family who is watching with me, "Oh well, we might as well turn it off now, because there's no way out. It's impossible." So, in the face of clear impossibility the most typical reaction is to become discouraged or fearful and give up.

When we view the mission of the church as difficult but doable, we may experience different levels of discouragement depending on just how difficult we see the mission before us. However, the Bible presents the mission of the church, not as difficult, but as impossible. So should we just throw in the towel? No. Because God has also promised--through the work of Christ and the Spirit--to do the impossible through his people as we put our faith to work. As we saw in the previous chapter, the Bible says that if we take a step of faith on the basis of who Christ is and what he has done, the most powerful force in the universe--the Holy Spirit--will flow out from us like mighty rivers to bring life and accomplish God's impossible mission.

> Now on the last day, the great day of the feast, Jesus stood and cried out, saying, "If anyone is thirsty, let him come to Me and drink. He who believes in Me, as the Scripture said, 'From his innermost being will flow rivers of living water.'" But this He spoke of the Spirit, whom those who believed in Him were to receive; for the Spirit was not yet given, because Jesus was not yet glorified.
> John 7:37-39 NASB 1995

So, God's people should be careful not to view the mission of the church as merely difficult. In that case, if we put our backs into it, maybe we can make some progress. We should rather recognize that the mission is impossible. There's no way we have the strength to carry it out. But in the face of the impossible, God's people should not become discouraged or fearful and give up. Rather we should believe God's promise and enthusiastically put our faith to work. Then he himself will do the impossible through us.

In any given situation, then, don't act on the basis of your fears and anxieties or pride. Rather, act on the basis of who God is, what

73

he has done in Christ and what he promises to do. That's how you put your faith to work, and that's when the Holy Spirit flows out from you to accomplish the impossible. Because the kingdom has already come, we should shamelessly ask for things in keeping with its full coming, impossible and outrageous though they may seem, and then be ready to be used of him to accomplish it.

Follow-up

1. In your daily life, do you tend to see the Christian life as easy? As difficult? As impossible? Give examples as evidence.

2. When was the last time you asked for something impossibly outrageous? What was it? How did you feel making that request? Why?

3. What specific things could you ask for that would be both in line with God's revealed will and outrageously impossible? Do it!

4. When was the last time you put your faith to work? Describe the situation and what it was like. Work at developing the habit of putting your faith to work. It might be helpful to keep a journal in this regard.

5. When was the last time you put your faith to work in prayer? Describe the situation and what it was like.

6. How do you feel the Heavenly Father feels about you? Do you see him as angry? Do you see him as loving and caring? Give evidence for your answer. Remind yourself of how much the Heavenly Father loves you and how eager he is to bless you.

Chapter 6

Pray with Boldness

My twelfth great grandfather, Dr. Rowland Taylor, was the fourth[1] martyr under the reign of Mary I, the queen of England and Ireland who put many godly men to death in her attempt to reverse the Reformation efforts of Henry VIII,[2] Edward VI and Thomas Cranmer Archbishop of Canterbury.[3]

Before Mary I came to power, Dr. Taylor had been given a position under Thomas Cranmer, who later appointed him Bishop of Hadleigh—a small rural town about 50 miles outside of London where he faithfully preached the Word of God and where the people of the town took God's Word very seriously as is evident from the following:

> .... a great number in that parish became exceedingly well learned
> in the holy Scriptures, as well women as men, so that a man might
> have found among them many that had often read the whole Bible
> through, and that could have said a great part of St. Paul's epistles
> by heart, and very well and readily have given a godly, learned
> sentence in any matter of controversy. Their children and servants
> were also brought up and trained so diligently in the right knowl-

edge of God's word, that the whole town seemed rather a university of the learned, than a town of cloth-making or labouring people. And, what is most to be commended, they were, for the most part, faithful followers of God's word in their living.[4]

At the end of his examination by Dr. Stephen Gardiner, Bishop of Winchester and Lord Chancellor, the Bishop threatened him in an attempt to get him to recant his belief that clergy should be able to marry, his rejection of transubstantiation, his belief in the sufficiency of Scripture, and his affirmation that only Christ is the head of the church. Taylor responded by kneeling down, lifting his hands and praying the following bold prayer:

> Good Lord, I thank thee; and from the tyranny of the Bishop of Rome, and all his detestable errors, idolatries, and abominations, good Lord, deliver us; and God be praised for good King Edward.[5]

Taylor was offered pardon if he would recant. In fact he was urged to recant. But he steadfastly refused. At one point he said,

> God be praised, since my condemnation I was never afraid to die.... Even from the bottom of my heart I am immoveable settled upon the rock, nothing doubting but that my dear God will perform and finish the work that he hath begun in me and others.[6]

His friends urged him to flee. They argued he would not get a fair hearing but would be put to death no matter what he said. He refused, asking them to pray this bold prayer: that

> God will give me strength and his Holy Spirit, that all mine adversaries shall have shame of their doings.[7]

Dr. Rowland Taylor was burned at the stake on February 9, 1555 for his refusal to recant truths that he found in the Bible. As I read his memoirs, it became clear to me that the Lord indeed answered his bold prayers. Certainly the way he behaved in the face of his condemnation had the opposite effect of that intended by those who decided to put him to death. His fearlessness in the face of his accusers, his willingness to face death in order to testify to the truth, his thoughtfulness to his family, friends and parishioners, his kindness to his jailers and the sheriffs charged with bringing him to his execution and carrying out the sentence impacted people in significant ways.

For example, to his wife and children he gave many encouraging words, including the following:

> Count me not dead, for I shall certainly live, and never die. I go
> before, and you follow after, to our long home.[8]

As Dr. Taylor was being brought by the sheriff and his men to his death, he carried on a friendly conversation with them, urging them to repent of their ungodly lifestyles. This moved them to tears and hopefully they did repent.[9] There is even some evidence that those who officially condemned him may have been put to shame by his unwavering testimony and Biblical rebukes. Stow relates the following reaction of Dr. Gardiner to Dr. Taylor's challenges to him:

> Thou art an arrogant knave, I see, and a very fool,' said Gardiner,
> sinking, before his bold rebuker, into weak and childish
> meanness.[10]

The point of this example from the life of Dr. Taylor is that prayer requires boldness because sometimes the answer to our prayers is not pleasant. Sometimes it can mean suffering and even death, as when Jesus prayed, "not my will but yours be done."[11] As agents of the kingdom, we should pray boldly for the fullness of the kingdom—no matter what the immediate consequences. Praying with boldness involves the courage to keep praying even in the face of discomfort, danger, and death. There is no place for fear—other than the fear of the Lord—among God's people in the Now-But-Not-Yet kingdom.

Habakkuk's journey from fear to bold prayer and faith will give us greater insight into the need for boldness in prayer. We learn from the book of Habakkuk that boldness requires (1) accepting the severity of God's judgment, (2) living by faith in God's promises, and (3) God's astonishing deeds.

The Severity of God's Judgment

Because we know God is gracious, there is a tendency to minimize the severity of his judgment. Our thinking tends to fall into the "balance paradigm" shown in Figure 6. We think that since God is gracious, surely his judgment would not be as severe as, for example, a negative 10 on the scale in Figure 1. Maybe a -5 or -6, but not a -10.

Figure 6. Unbiblical Balance View of Judgment and Promise

This is the same error into which Habakkuk had fallen. In Habakkuk 1:2-4 the prophet complains that God's people have not been judged for their sin, which has gotten out of hand. If only God would judge them, there would be a revival of God's people. However, when in 1:5-11 God replies that he is indeed going to judge his people, but in a way that Habakkuk would never have believed possible, Habakkuk complains that the judgment is too severe (1:13). God says,

> "Look among the nations! Observe! Be astonished! Wonder! Because I am doing something[12] in your days— You would not believe if you were told.

Habakkuk 1:5 NASB 1995

What is this amazing work of God? He is going to send the Babylonian army against God's people. Habakkuk knows how ruthless they are and how they are bent on worldwide domination. He is afraid that God's people will be wiped off the map.

The historical background to this event will help clarify how Habakkuk felt. God had made clear to Abraham that God's full judgment must fall by ordering him to sacrifice his son Isaac--the one through whom all of God's promises were to be fulfilled (Genesis 22). If Isaac were to die, there would be no hope of the promises being fulfilled. But Abraham trusted that God would indeed fulfill his promises, and that, if necessary, God would raise Isaac from the dead (Hebrews 11:19). At the last moment, God stopped Abraham from sacrificing his son, and provided a substitute--a ram.

When God rescued his people from slavery in Egypt, there were probably about 2 million people who came out. They had been spared from God's judgment in the plagues when in faith that God would provide a substitute, they sacrificed a lamb and placed its blood at the entry way to their homes. God brought them, as promised, to the land of Canaan. But when they got to the border and heard the report of the spies that there were giants in the land, they refused to go in and take the land (Numbers 14:1-4). God said to Moses that he was going to destroy them and start over (Numbers 14:11-12). But Moses, anticipating the mediatorial role of Christ, asked God for mercy (Numbers 14:13-19). God did grant mercy in the form of a partial judgment: those who were at least 20 years old would die in the desert, while those who were younger would enter the promised land (Numbers 14:29). This partial judgment might resemble the balance view of Figure 1 in that the full judgment was withheld because of God's mercy. But this partial judgment is different in that the full judgment still awaits. The partial judgment is only a temporary solution.

But this wasn't the last time God used it. When the 10 northern tribes of Israel rejected God, he sent them into captivity at the hands of the Assyrians. They never returned. So, the number of the multitude of people that left Egypt was being severely reduced through God's method of partial judgment. It was in this situation that Habakkuk heard that God was going to send the Babylonian army against the remaining tribes of Israel--now referred to as Judah. No doubt he was hoping for the kind of judgment--not too harsh-- that would allow Judah to return to the glory that had been theirs under the rules of King David and King Solomon. But now with the news from God about the Babylonians coming, these hopes were dashed. The numbers of God's people would not only be reduced further, but they were likely to be obliterated. God was telling Habakkuk that the method of partial judgment could not be used indefinitely. At some point the full judgment must fall. Under these circumstances, Habakkuk was afraid. He says,

> I heard and my inward parts trembled, At the sound my lips quivered. Decay enters my bones, And in my place I tremble.
> Habakkuk 3:16 NASB 1995[13]

Habakkuk also prays,

> In wrath remember mercy.
> Habakkuk 3:2 NASB 1995

When bad things happen to us, we tend to think along these lines: "Why did God allow this to happen to me? What did I do to deserve this?" And let me hasten to add that not every bad thing that happens to God's people is punishment for some specific sin[14], as in the case of God's sending the Babylonians against Judah. Sometimes we suffer just because we've been faithful, and the Lord is giving us an opportunity to exercise our faith. Other times we suffer just because we belong to Christ. In any case, all this suffering comes in one way or another as a result of the fall. The book of Habakkuk reminds us of just what we do deserve: the fullness of God's wrath against sin. Yes, our sin is worse than we often think it is and requires more drastic measures than we would often like to admit. God wants us to be willing to give up our lives--to give up all for the sake of the kingdom.

But if we give up all, will we be disappointed? Will our hopes be dashed? No, because God's promises are greater than we can imagine.

Living by Faith in God's Promises

The book of Habakkuk contrasts living by faith with what I call living by points. Living by points means that your sense of worth is wrapped up in having what you and/or your society values. It's as if one's culture hands out points--rewards--to those who buy into its standards. The more points you have, the more important you are considered to be. Something like this is what the apostle Paul meant when he said,

> Therefore from now on we recognize no one according to the flesh; even though we have known Christ according to the flesh, yet now we know Him in this way no longer. Therefore if anyone is in Christ, he is a new creature; the old things passed away; behold, new things have come.
> 2 Corinthians 5:14-17 NASB 1995

Evaluating people "according to the flesh" is evaluating them from the perspective of the world and what it has to offer apart from Christ and the new creation that comes through him. Physical beauty, a commanding presence, education, titles, special abilities, lots of *things* and comforts--none of these is bad in itself. It's not necessarily wrong to have points. In Philippians 3:5-6 the apostle Paul lists some of the cultural points assigned to him by his culture[15]. In addition to these, he was a Roman citizen, and even made use of this fact for the sake of his ministry[16]. On the other hand, when we *live* by these things, we are not living by faith. Paul says he counts the points assigned to him by his culture as rubbish in comparison with knowing Christ. What is valued may change somewhat from culture to culture and from person to person, but in the end living by points means finding your sense of importance in something created. This is what the Bible means when it uses the word idolatry.

The king of Babylon lived by points, as shown in the following verses.

"Behold, as for the proud one, His soul is not right within him; But the righteous will live by his faith. "Furthermore, wine betrays the haughty man, So that he does not stay at home. He enlarges his appetite like Sheol, And he is like death, never satisfied. He also gathers to himself all nations And collects to himself all peoples.
Habakkuk 2:4-5 NASB 1995

The king of Babylon was after more than most people: he wanted world domination. He was on a mission to gain more societal points than anyone. This is idolatry and doomed to failure, according to the book of Habakkuk.

What profit is the idol when its maker has carved it, Or an image, a teacher of falsehood? For its maker trusts in his own handiwork When he fashions speechless idols. Woe to him who says to a piece of wood, 'Awake!' To a mute stone, 'Arise!' And that is your teacher? Behold, it is overlaid with gold and silver, And there is no breath at all inside it. "But the Lord is in His holy temple. Let all the earth be silent before Him.
Habakkuk 2:18-20 NASB 1995

The king of Babylon trusts his own power to gain world domination. What good is world domination even if you achieve it if in the end you die and lose it all? And even if you achieve what you want, in the end it will not satisfy the longings of your heart. Idols cannot give you what you really want. They are lifeless and speechless. But the Lord is not speechless. He has important, life-giving things to say. We should stop working so hard to find something to satisfy us and listen to him.

> Is it not indeed from the Lord of hosts that peoples toil for fire, And nations grow weary for nothing?
>   Habakkuk 2:13 NASB 1995

World domination is nothing compared to what God has in store for his people. For although the nations exhaust themselves for nothing,

> .... the earth will be filled with the knowledge of the glory of the Lord, As the waters cover the sea.
>   Habakkuk 2:14 NASB 1995

God says, in effect, to Habakkuk, "Don't be empty and grasping for something to fill you up, like the King of Babylon. Don't cling to a vision of returning to the glory of David's reign. I have a much greater glory in store for you." In fact,

> "Things which eye has not seen and ear has not heard, And which have not entered the heart of man, All that God has prepared for those who love Him."
>   1 Corinthians 2:9 NASB 1995

But the Bible does give us a few hints about the coming glory. We will have new bodies that don't depend on the energy from the sun and that don't need to recuperate energy by sleeping. There will be no death and no sin. We will live on a renewed earth and God will live in our midst. I imagine one of the things we might do is explore and go on important missions in God's incredible and renewed cosmos.

Living by faith in God's promise is much better than living by points. The book of Habakkuk specifically contrasts living by points with living by faith. Referring to the King of Babylon as "the proud one" it says,

> "Behold, as for the proud one, His soul is not right within him; But the righteous will live by his faith.
> Habakkuk 2:4 NASB 1995

Instead of living by points, we should believe God's promises and be willing if necessary to give up all points--even to the point of death.[17] This is what it means to live by faith. When we set our hopes on and spend our energies on less than what God has promised--like being content with the praise of others, or with other kinds of societal points, we are not living by faith. Rather, we have become captivated by the culture. Living by faith means believing the great promises of God even in the face of the loss of all points—death itself.

Yes, it's true that God's judgment is more severe than we often think. But it's also true that his promises go beyond our wildest dreams. He who believes is on a mission--not to gain points, but to point others to God's astonishing deeds.

God's Astonishing Deeds

A minimized view of God's judgment, along with a minimized view of his promises, tend to lock each other in place, making us captives of the culture with its point system, and limiting our missional impact. What is it that can rescue us? God's astonishing deeds. As Habakkuk contemplates the coming judgment of God at the hands of the Babylonians, he launches into a prayer in verse one of chapter three that continues to the end of the book. He prays,

Lord, I have heard the report about You and I fear. O Lord, revive Your work in the midst of the years, In the midst of the years make it known; In wrath remember mercy.

Habakkuk 3:2[18] NASB 1995

God's deeds as shown in the history of Israel are astonishing. In verse 3 of chapter 3, Habakkuk recites examples from the past as part of his prayer. Here are a few lines:

God comes from Teman.... Before Him goes pestilence, And plague comes after Him. He stood and surveyed the earth; He looked and startled the nations.... In indignation You marched through the earth; In anger You trampled the nations. You went forth for the salvation of Your people, For the salvation of Your anointed.... You trampled on the sea with Your horses, On the surge of many waters.

Habakkuk 3:3-15 NASB 1995

There are obvious references here to the Exodus, when God rescued his people from slavery in Egypt. Habakkuk calls on God to renew these astonishing works. Judgment must fall even on God's people, but Habakkuk prays that God will somehow combine that judgment with his astonishing deeds to rescue his people.

By the end of his book, we see that Habakkuk has moved from fear to faith. He isn't looking forward to the coming of the Babylonians. In fact, he trembles in fear of the Lord when he thinks about God's promised judgment on his people. He continues his prayer:

I heard and my inward parts trembled, At the sound my lips quivered. Decay enters my bones, And in my place I tremble. Because I must wait quietly for the day of distress, For the people to arise who will invade us.

Habakkuk 3:16 NASB 1995

But after remembering God's astonishing works in the past, he is willing to give up all if necessary and trust God to fulfill his promise that the just will live by faith, even when things look impossibly hopeless. He prays boldly, now addressing God in the third person,[19]

Though the fig tree should not blossom And there be no fruit on the vines, Though the yield of the olive should fail And the fields produce no food, Though the flock should be cut off from the fold And there be no cattle in the stalls, Yet I will exult in the Lord, I will rejoice in the God of my salvation.
Habakkuk 3:17-18 NASB 1995

The situation he describes here is a hopeless one. There is no food. Everyone would be expected to die. Yet he rejoices in God who has promised to take care of his people and make them live. It is a very bold expression of faith in prayer. In the final verse of the book, we get a vision of fearlessness. Habakkuk says,

The Lord God is my strength, And He has made my feet like hinds' feet, And makes me walk on my high places.
Habakkuk 3:19 NASB 1995

A deer on the heights is above his predators. He has the high ground and can defend himself. Habakkuk was moved from fear to bold faith even though he wasn't sure how God would renew his awesome deeds. He was moved from fear to faith in the face of looming judgment. His bold prayer echoed the words of Job:

Though He slay me, I will hope in Him.
Job 13:15 NASB 1995

Did God answer Habakkuk's prayer? Well, the Babylonians did come, just as God had said. They destroyed the temple. Homes were destroyed, people died, the land was devastated. Many were taken captive and brought to Babylon. After 70 years of captivity, only a remnant returned to the land. Clearly God's method of partial judgment is still in operation. The two million people that came out of Egypt is now but a remnant.

After the return of the remnant, it becomes clear that the judgment they received was not enough to deal with the sin in their hearts. They kept living by points instead of living by faith. They were more interested in rebuilding their own homes than in rebuilding God's temple. They were more interested in their own comfort than in giving a tithe of their income to the Lord. So where was the astonishing work of the Lord?

Eventually the Romans came and took control of the land. By now Israel was clearly not the head but the tail of the nations.[20] There were some Jews, called Zealots, who still held out hope that they could overthrow the Romans and return to the glory days of David and Solomon. Even the twelve disciples tended to buy into the vision of the overthrow of Roman domination, with themselves sitting on twelves thrones judging Israel. This was their cultural frame of reference. They tended to interpret Jesus' words within this frame, thus expecting him to take the lead in the overthrow of Rome. The nation of Israel was about to disappear, but the disciples held out hope that the full judgment of God would not fall before Jesus rescued them from Rome and made them once again the head of the nations.

The nation of Israel was a "smoldering wick" about to be snuffed out. But Isaiah had made this prophecy about the Messiah:

A bruised reed He will not break And a dimly burning wick He will not extinguish;
    Isaiah 42:3 NASB 1995

Indeed, Jesus was gentle with the disciples. He would not allow the full judgment of God to fall on them. They would not be obliterated, even though they deserved it with all their arguments about who had more points. God's program of partial judgment had led to this time in which Israel was at the point of disappearing. There is a sense, then, in which Jesus was the last one of God's people left. If God continued with this program just a little longer, they would all be gone. Jesus came in the nick of time.

How did he rescue them? Not by overthrowing the Romans. No, he rescued them by suffering himself the full wrath of God that Israel had deserved all these years. He himself came to be the true sacrificial lamb that would suffer, not a partial judgment, but the full judgment of God against all of his people. In the Garden of Gethsemane, the disciples left Jesus alone as they fell asleep. Meanwhile, Jesus faced with great sadness the task before him. He asked the Father if there was any other way to accomplish his purposes.

Unlike Habakkuk, who when he heard about the coming of the Babylonians was filled with fear, Jesus was fearless as he faced a much greater judgment. Yes, he was sad--unto death (Matthew 26:38). No doubt the fear of the Lord gave him wisdom. But he was not afraid. In the face of God's full judgment against the sin of God's people, Jesus is our fearless leader. He prayed with great boldness:

.... yet not My will, but Yours be done.
Luke 22:42 NASB 1995

In other words, "I'm willing to face hell on behalf of my people if that is your will."

And since Jesus lived by faith in the Father, and not by points, the promise that the just will live by faith was shown to be true. He trusted the Father in the face of death, and the Father made him live. He brought him back to life.

Yes, God has renewed his awesome deeds, just as Habakkuk had prayed. He has renewed them in the person and work of Jesus Christ the Messiah. And now, those who live by faith in Christ--and not by points--will also live.

This means that we also, like our leader, should be fearless. How much more should we who have seen the great renewal in Christ of his awesome deeds be fearless! We who live by faith in Christ and not by points are seated with him in the heavenly realms--on the heights. We have every reason to be fearless and to pray with boldness.

There are movies in which the hero for some reason--in some cases the loss of a loved spouse-- is no longer afraid to die. He is not afraid to die because life is no longer worth living. This makes him a formidable force for good in the movie. How much more can we who have already died with Christ and have every reason to live for him be used of the Lord to bring about his kingdom purposes as we fearlessly live by faith in him!

If we want to see God's power unleashed among his people, we've got to stop being impressed by the points the American dream can offer, stop fearing the loss of it, and be astonished once again by the work of God in Christ.

Praying with Boldness

The judgment that Habakkuk feared has now fallen on Christ. So, we have nothing to fear. However, in this Now-But-Not-Yet kingdom we have the privilege of participating in the sufferings of Christ. We walk the way of the cross.[21] We are supposed to be soldiers willing to give up our lives—along with all societal points—for the sake of the kingdom.

The Lord had healed a cripple through Peter and John. The Jewish leaders threatened them not to speak any more in Jesus' name. Peter and John told these leaders they had murdered God's Anointed. They insisted they would not stop speaking in Jesus' name. Then they went to tell the church what had happened. All the believers joined together in bold prayer for boldness:

> When they had been released, they went to their own companions and reported all that the chief priests and the elders had said to them. And when they heard this, they lifted their voices to God

with one accord and said, "O Lord, it is You who made the heaven and the earth and the sea, and all that is in them, who by the Holy Spirit, through the mouth of our father David Your servant, said,

'Why did the Gentiles rage, And the peoples devise futile things? 'The kings of the earth took their stand, And the rulers were gathered together Against the Lord and against His Christ.' For truly in this city there were gathered together against Your holy servant Jesus, whom You anointed, both Herod and Pontius Pilate, along with the Gentiles and the peoples of Israel, to do whatever Your hand and Your purpose predestined to occur. And now, Lord, take note of their threats, and grant that Your bond-servants may speak Your word with all confidence, while You extend Your hand to heal, and signs and wonders take place through the name of Your holy servant Jesus."

Acts 4: 23-30 NASB 1995

Notice that they didn't pray for protection—although it would not have been wrong to do so. Surely their safety must have been on their minds. Stephen had been killed for the same kinds of "offenses." But that wasn't what was foremost in their minds. They prayed rather for boldness to speak God's Word, and for God to confirm their word through mighty works. And God answered their prayer immediately.

And when they had prayed, the place where they had gathered together was shaken, and they were all filled with the Holy Spirit and began to speak the word of God with boldness.

Acts 4:31 NASB 1995

Cowardly prayers are those that are conditioned by a deep-seated desire for societal points. Bold prayers are those that desire the kingdom even above one's health and life. It's not wrong, of course, to pray for health and life. But we should ask ourselves *why* we pray for these things.

We are to pray for the kingdom with boldness even in the face of mountainous obstacles that can make us tremble and threaten to undo us. We do so because the kingdom has already come in Christ and because the fullness of the kingdom is guaranteed by the outpouring of the Spirit and the session[22] of Christ at the right hand of the Father. God's kingdom power has been unleashed and the proper response is bold prayer: Your kingdom come no matter what it means for me now! Jesus said,

> Truly, truly, I say to you, if you ask the Father for anything in My name, He will give it to you.
> John 16:23 NASB 1995

An assumption behind this prayer is faith that in spite of the suffering and death that involvement in the kingdom may bring, God will make us live. In other words, "whatever you ask" implies the following: "if you want the kingdom so badly that you are willing to give up all and entrust yourself to the one who promises to make you live." The question is, "do we want the full coming of his kingdom more than we want good circumstances?" Do we want it more than we want comfort? Is our desire for the kingdom limited by our fears? Is boldness in prayer limited by a deep-seated desire for societal points, and a consequent fear that they will be taken away?

Pray boldly and without fear because God in Christ has overcome death and hell and is working all things together for the good of his people. God's people have every reason to be the most courageous people on earth.

* * *

Follow-up

1. When difficult and challenging circumstances enter your life, do you find yourself asking, "Why did God allow this to happen to me? What did I do to deserve this?" If so, how do you evaluate this response?
2. Are you bold in prayer?
3. When you read the previous question, was your tendency to minimize your boldness in order not to sound proud? If so, what does that say about your understanding of boldness?
4. When you become a believer, you're saying in effect, "I'm willing to die for the cause." This should increasingly make us bold and fearless as we grow and understand its implications. Do you see yourself as being willing to give up all for the sake of the kingdom? Explain your answer. Boldness grows as we are willing to give up all.
5. Do your prayers reflect your willingness to give up all for the sake of the kingdom? Give examples either way.
6. In what ways do you see yourself tempted to live by points instead of living by faith? Do you see this reflected in your prayers? If so, how?
7. In what ways do you see your church tempted to live by points instead of living by faith? Do you see this reflected in prayer? If so, how?
8. How do you evaluate this statement: "God's people have every reason to be the most courageous people on earth"? Is he making you courageous? Explain your answer.

Chapter 7

Pray with Humility

M any years ago I was in a conference of missionary leaders from across the globe. In one of the sessions, the teacher was trying to convince us that we were not "broken" and humble leaders. He referred us to David's words in Psalm 51:17 about having "a broken spirit, a broken and a contrite heart." I'm not sure how he could know this about each and every one of us, but I suspect it was because he didn't see in us what he considered to be the evidence of being broken: taking every opportunity to tell stories about how sinful you are[1] and never saying anything positive about yourself and what the Lord is doing in your life. He put a lot of psychological pressure on us to stop resisting and "be broken." This included him telling many stories about how sinful he was.

If I had heard his presentation 15 years earlier I would have readily accepted it. Back then I had been morbidly introspective, trying very hard in my own strength to "be humble" and "be spiritual." I spent 2-3 hours daily in Bible reading and prayer—and of course it's good to read the Bible and pray—but[2] to a large extent my motives were self-centered. I was looking for a "method" that would make me feel spiritual. Advertising my sin and suppressing what the Lord was doing in my life would certainly have been a method I could have carried out. I'm sure I was a Christian at that time, but I needed to understand more deeply the implications of the gospel.

In any case, as I listened to this man's presentation, I felt like he was trying to throw me back into the mode of morbid introspection from with the Lord had delivered me. As I listened to him pressure us, I had a good conscience before the Lord. I regularly examined myself as the apostle Paul says to do,[3] and was sure that the Lord would gradually reveal to me the greater depths of my sin at the appropriate times. In the meantime, I knew I was forgiven. Could I say I was humble? Yes, maybe I could even say that!

Humility according to the Bible is seeing yourself the way God does. For believers in Christ, that includes being willing to admit our sin as we become aware of it, and also acknowledging what the Lord has done and is continuing to do in one's life. I think it's difficult for Christians to pray with humility because of the unbiblical views of humility that surround us.

The Unbiblical Balance View of Humility

Our culture tends to view humility as the opposite of boldness and courage. Humility is attributed to people who allow themselves to be taken advantage of—as if they were a carpet to be stepped on. A typical dictionary definition of humility is "a modest or low view of one's own importance." When I was in college, I drew a more primitive version of the diagram found in Figure 7 as I first began to struggle with this issue in earnest. The diagram is meant to illustrate our culture's erroneous version of humility.

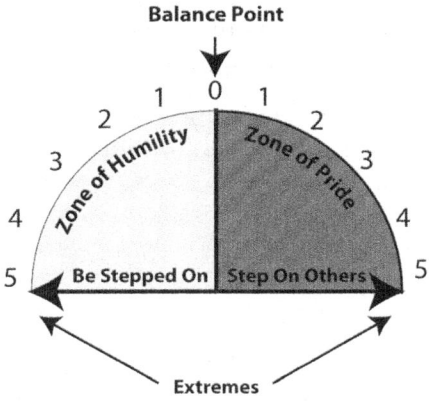

Figure 7. Typical but Unbiblical View of Humility

According to this diagram, humility means not speaking up, denying one's gifts and abilities, and letting people do things their way. The supposed "good" side of this kind of humility is that you aren't stepping on other people. The "bad" side is that you can't be yourself. Pride also has an apparent "good" side: you aren't letting people walk all over you. But the "bad" side is that you end up stepping on other people.

According to this line of thinking, then, you don't want to be either too humble or too proud. The humbler you are the more you will be stepped on by others. The prouder you are, the more you will step on others. Following this logic, the ideal spot is the "balance point." This *mean between the extremes*, while it reduces the "bad" side of both, also diminishes the "good" side of both. This kind of balance—a mean between the extremes—is not a Christian solution. This unbiblical worldview is presented in the trilogy *The Hunger Games*[4] By the end of the trilogy, this view emerges: you are either a victim being stepped on and used by others, or you are victimizing and stepping on other people.[5] In this unbiblical worldview, there is no other alternative.

Sadly, the idea of "balance" is used frequently even in many

Bible-believing churches to explain not only humility but the dynamics of Christian living in general. Even though many churches know the fruit of the Spirit is a supernaturally produced gift from God, when they explain how to *get* humility they often resort to the idea of balance.[6]

The Fear of Pride

There is a tendency in many church circles today to assume that being humble means you never talk about yourself in what might be considered a positive way. Biblical self-denial is interpreted to be a denial of the gifts, abilities, and personality the Lord has given us. According to this mentality, it's perfectly acceptable to talk about how sinful and weak you are, but not about the gifts the Lord has given you or what he has done through you. Nor is it acceptable, according to this way of thinking, to defend yourself against criticism or to criticize others. Talking about your own growth in the Lord is not considered to be humble. These are all considered to be prideful actions.

However, the apostle Paul did all of these things. Here are just a few examples:

1. Brethren, I have lived my life with a perfectly good conscience before God up to this day. (Acts 23:1)
2. But to me it is a very small thing that I may be examined by you, or by any human court. (1 Corinthians 4:3)
3. Be imitators of me, just as I also am of Christ. (1 Corinthians 11:1. See also Philippians 3:17))
4. Yet we do speak wisdom among those who are mature. (1 Corinthians 2:6)
5. But we will not boast beyond our measure, but within the measure of the sphere which God apportioned to us as a measure, to reach even as far as you. (2 Corinthians 10:13)

6. But even if I am unskilled in speech, yet I am not so in knowledge; in fact, in every way we have made this evident to you in all things. (2 Corinthians 11:6)
7. I consider that I am not in the least inferior to these super-apostles. (2 Corinthians 11:6 ESV)
8. Such men are false apostles. (2 Corinthians 11:13 ESV)
9. For God is my witness, how I long for you all with the affection of Christ Jesus. (Philippians 1:8)
10. But whatever things were gain to me, those things I have counted as loss for the sake of Christ. More than that, I count all things to be loss in view of the surpassing value of knowing Christ Jesus my Lord, for whom I have suffered the loss of all things, and count them but rubbish so that I may gain Christ.... (Philippians 3:7-8)
11. Let us therefore, as many as are perfect, have this attitude; and if in anything you have a different attitude, God will reveal that also to you; (Philippians 3:15)
12. Brethren, I do not regard myself as having laid hold of it yet; but one thing I do: forgetting what lies behind and reaching forward to what lies ahead, I press on toward the goal for the prize of the upward call of God in Christ Jesus. (Philippians 3:13-14)
13. According to the grace of God which was given to me, like a wise master builder I laid a foundation, and another is building on it. (1 Corinthians 3:10)
14. Let a man regard us in this manner, as servants of Christ and stewards of the mysteries of God. (1 Corinthians 4:1, See also 9:17)
15. For if you were to have countless tutors in Christ, yet you would not have many fathers, for in Christ Jesus I became your father through the gospel. (1 Corinthians 4:15)
16. I thank God, I speak in tongues more than you all; (1 Corinthians 14:18)

17. But by the grace of God I am what I am, and His grace toward me did not prove vain; but I labored even more than all of them, yet not I, but the grace of God with me. (1 Corinthians 15:10)

Of course, in 2 Corinthians 10 and following, Paul is making an unusual defense of his ministry. He calls his defense "foolishness." However, he deems this "foolishness" necessary given the situation. Believers should take seriously his example.

Paul even goes so far as to say he is humble:

...serving the Lord with all humility....
　　Acts 20:19 NASB 1995

In expressing this he was imitating Christ, who said,

I am gentle and humble in heart....
　　Matthew 11:29 NASB 1995

I've heard it said that you can't *say* you are humble and still *be* humble. In other words, saying you are humble is an act of pride, according to these people. Obviously, the apostle disagrees.

Paul also says this:

But each one must examine his own work, and then he will have reason for boasting in regard to himself alone, and not in regard to another.
　　Galatians 6:4 NASB 1995

What did he say? Boasting in yourself? About this verse William Hendriksen says that a person:

should mirror himself in the mirror of God's law and of Christ's example. If, after doing this, there is still room for making any claims—as there may be, indeed!—then the possibilities of glorying will have arisen from himself, that is, from that which God has accomplished in his heart, not from comparing himself with someone else.[7]

In other words, it is legitimate to boast about what the Lord has done in and through you, and about the gifts he has given you. After all, it's all by his grace.

The passages listed above used to really bother me because it seemed to me that Paul was being prideful. I found similar disturbing statements from the mouth of David.[8] I began to see, however, that I was viewing these actions from the posture of a kind of false humility, which always interprets gospel boldness as pride. Part of being humble is recognizing the gifts the Lord has given you and expressing what he has done in your life.

Of course, this can be done in a prideful way. It's true that many times people who talk about themselves are being proud. But the way to avoid pride isn't to stop recognizing and expressing what the Lord has done for you. That's a fleshly maneuver. It is being fearful of *coming across* as proud. The concern for one's image is at center stage. The image projections involved in the fear of coming across as proud are just as sinful as blatant pride.

Being humble while at the same time making the kinds of bold statements that Paul makes, without a doubt requires the power of the Spirit. When we "boast" about what the Lord has done through us, it should always be with a spirit of humility and thankfulness. Trying to avoid pride by refraining from certain kinds of statements and actions is disempowering. Lord have mercy on us who have been captivated by the fear of pride.

Praying with humility means praying with a keen awareness of who we are in Christ. For example, when we pray with humility, we pray as those who by grace have been given eternal life, who are forgiven, who are citizens of the kingdom of God, in whom God lives by his Holy Spirit, who have been made heirs with Christ of all

things, who are dearly loved by God, who are kingdom agents on a
mission, who still struggle with sin, who need to daily confess our
sins, who are disciplined by God for our good, who do not live by
social points but by faith.

Bold Humility

In his book *The Fruit of the Spirit*,[9] John Sanderson says that
humility is not the opposite of courage and boldness. In fact, it takes
courage to be humble in an evil world. Rather, the opposite of
humility is self-centeredness. We are to deny the defensive attitude
that shows an insecurity with who we are. If a concern for humility
leads us to minimize the use of our gifts, then we have misunderstood humility and hindered the mission to which we have been
called.

True humility is always accompanied by a gospel boldness that is
zealous to see God's name glorified and his kingdom come in its fullness. This bold humility that is produced by the Spirit through the
gospel does not hold back on the use of one's gifts for fear of coming
across as proud. In fact, the Bible makes it clear that every gift given
by the Lord is necessary for the building up of the body of Christ. We
might even say that the withholding of our gifts is a kind of self-
centeredness: we are more concerned about our image[10] than about
God's glory and kingdom.

We often find it difficult to distinguish between gospel boldness
and pride. We also find it difficult to distinguish between true
humility and the spineless fear of standing up for anything or the fear
of moving forward. It isn't hard for God though. To him they are like
the difference between night and day. And the only reason we can't
see the difference clearly is because of our lack of growth and the fog
that the sin in our flesh produces. But the more we get to know Jesus,
the more we become like him, and the more we are able to distinguish
between the two.

During Jesus' ministry he used his gifts and abilities to the fullest.

However, he did not do these things to call attention to himself. Isaiah prophesied about him,

> He will not cry out or raise His voice, Nor make His voice heard in the street.
> Isaiah 42:2 NASB 1995

He had no insecurity that led him to make a name for himself. He wasn't interested in glorifying himself, but in bringing glory to his Father. Furthermore, because he was secure, he was able to be gentle with others. Again, as Isaiah prophesied,

> A bruised reed He will not break And a dimly burning wick He will not extinguish;
> Isaiah 42:3 NASB 1995

Israel was a bruised reed and a smoldering wick. And while they deserved eternal punishment, Jesus was gentle with them. Rather than call down fire from heaven, he preached the good news of the kingdom, healed, and warned.

To the extent that we see in ourselves the bold humility produced by the gospel, it will be the result of the gospel opening our eyes to see ourselves the way the Lord sees us: redeemed sinners still affected by the flesh, and empowered children of God with an important role in his kingdom. Bold humility leads us to use our gifts with zeal, while at the same time being eager to learn from others—because it's only together with all the saints that we will be able to understand what is otherwise beyond understanding: all the dimensions of Christ's love.[11]

Because of our continual struggle with the flesh,[12] and because there is always more room for growth in the Lord, our ability to distinguish between pride and boldness on the one hand and between humility and fear on the other, will never be perfect. But it's our direction of growth either toward or away from the Lord that counts the most. Even a small child can have bold humility, as when he or she says with complete confidence, "Don't worry, Daddy; Jesus will take care of us."

Praying with Bold Humility

Praying boldly is not the opposite of praying with humility. They go together. Jesus modeled the humility of kingdom prayer when in the Garden of Gethsemane, as he faced his coming death, he said,

> Father, if You are willing, remove this cup from Me; yet not My will, but Yours be done.
> Luke 22:42 NASB 1995

As Jesus submitted to the will of the Father, so we are also commanded to pray,

> Your will be done, on earth as it is in heaven.
> Matthew 6:10 NASB 1995

Although God wants us to take initiative and is interested in our ideas, requests, praise, confessions of sin and thankfulness, prayer is not a *manipulation* of God to do things according to our timetable or in the particular ways we think best. Neither is prayer a way to project an image of spiritual maturity to those with whom we pray. God does not answer based on our merit or our many and eloquent words, as the Pharisee thought, as if God were indebted to us for our having fulfilled some duty. In this case, the tax collector had it right:

> But the tax collector, standing some distance away, was even unwilling to lift up his eyes to heaven, but was beating his breast, saying, 'God, be merciful to me, the sinner!' I tell you, this man went to his house justified rather than the other; for everyone who

exalts himself will be humbled, but he who humbles himself will be exalted."

Luke 18:13-14 NASB 1995

Yes, we pray boldly, but in the midst of a profound sense of both our weakness and inadequacy and our grace-bestowed status in Christ. God brings about the implications of the work of Christ as his people rely on him rather than on the gifts he has given us--like evangelism or preaching, or the ability to relate well to others. Trusting Christ requires that we combine the use of these gifts with humble prayer. God hears the prayer of the broken-hearted who cry out to him and who with humble boldness insist on the fullness of his promises, only because of what he has done in Christ and promises to do.

Follow-up

1. Do you think it's possible for someone to say he's humble without being proud? Explain your answer.
2. Does your culture see humility as being the opposite of courageous? Explain your answer by giving examples.
3. Do you typically see humility as the opposite of courageous? Give some examples either way.
4. Are you hesitant to use your gifts for fear of being labeled proud? Explain your answer through examples.
5. Are you hesitant to pray with boldness for fear of being perceived as proud? Explain.
6. Have you experienced praying as one who is weak and brokenhearted? Describe your experience either way.

7. Have you experienced prayer that is both humble and bold? If so, explain what that was like. If not, how do you feel about that?

8. Is there anything in this chapter that encourages you to pray with bold humility? Explain.

Chapter 8

Pray Earnestly

Wanting the Kingdom

It's well known among consultants of Organizational Development that your consulting will rarely be successful if the company or group asking for your help doesn't want it badly enough to be willing to make more than a few tweaks here and there.

Whenever I consult with churches or missionary teams, I try to make sure up front that the decision-makers really want me to come, and that, if necessary, they are willing to make significant changes. If they are not willing to take the necessary time, and provide the necessary resources, then they're probably not taking it seriously enough to make a difference. If they're looking for some kind of magic formula or insight that will suddenly and without much effort, persistence, self-examination, involvement and change bring about great effectiveness and growth, it's usually better not to take the time to try to help them.

So also, the Lord Jesus wants to help us his people be effective kingdom agents. But he also wants to know how much we want it. Are we earnest or half-hearted? The Bible says,

> You do not have because you do not ask.
> James 4:2 NASB 1995

In other words, "You must not really want what I have to offer. You say you want it, but you must have other competing motives that are winning out."

Jesus says belonging to the kingdom is of inestimable value so that we should want it more than anything else:

> The kingdom of heaven is like a treasure hidden in the field, which a man found and hid again; and from joy over it he goes and sells all that he has and buys that field.
> Matthew 13:44 NASB 1995

We pray earnestly for the fullness of the kingdom because it's like a pearl of great price. It's like a treasure that you find hidden in a field. These are so valuable that, according to Jesus, you go and sell everything you have in order to get them[1]. How much do you want to be part of the kingdom? How much do you want the fullness of the kingdom to come? To what extent have you been captivated by the point system of your society? Are you willing to give up everything else, if necessary, in order to have the kingdom? James points out our tendency to lack earnestness in prayer because of "double-mindedness." He says:

> Consider it all joy, my brethren, when you encounter various trials, knowing that the testing of your faith produces endurance. And let endurance have its perfect result, so that you may be perfect and complete, lacking in nothing. But if any of you lacks wisdom, let him ask of God, who gives to all generously and without reproach, and it will be given to him. But he must ask in faith without any

doubting, for the one who doubts is like the surf of the sea, driven and tossed by the wind. For that man ought not to expect that he will receive anything from the Lord, being a double-minded man, unstable in all his ways.

James 1:2-8 NASB 1995

James asks the recipients of this letter (and us as well), to look at trials from a different perspective. Yes, they are painful, and yes, they make us less acceptable and less important according to our culture's value system. But on the other hand, they come from God's hand and are extremely valuable. They are "exercises" provided by God. I use this word "exercises" because Hebrews 12:11 ("those who have been trained[2]" by it) refers to hardship and suffering as training from God-- the kind of training an athlete would receive in order to excel at his sport. This is part of the challenging adventure we discussed in Chapter 3. God trains us for excellence in his kingdom by giving us opportunities to put our faith in him to work. We don't know what our faith can do until it is tested. An athlete who gives up halfway through the sports event needs more training. God's training produces perseverance. It also makes us "mature and complete, not lacking anything." His training woos us away from the enticement of our societal point systems, and to the glory of the King and his king-dom. He thus makes us increasingly useful in his kingdom.

James also says that if you don't have enough wisdom to be able to see your trials from God's training perspective, you should ask him for that wisdom. He will gladly give it to you. James adds that if after asking you don't receive it, it's not because God isn't willing to give it to you but because you don't really want it that badly. You are half-hearted or double-minded. You lack earnestness. You want to grow in kingdom usefulness, but you also want other things. The allure of your societal point system makes you waver. You are torn between the two.[3]

So, the Bible tells us to ask, seek and knock, thus indicating a required persistence and insistence that reveal our earnestness.

Ask, and it will be given to you; seek, and you will find; knock, and it will be opened to you. For everyone who asks receives, and he who seeks finds, and to him who knocks it will be opened.

Matthew 7:7-8 NASB 1995

We are to be like the widow who wore out the judge with her asking until he finally gave in. He knew she really wanted justice and wasn't going to give up.

Now He was telling them a parable to show that at all times they ought to pray and not to lose heart, saying, "In a certain city there was a judge who did not fear God and did not respect man. There was a widow in that city, and she kept coming to him, saying, 'Give me legal protection from my opponent.' For a while he was unwilling; but afterward he said to himself, 'Even though I do not fear God nor respect man, yet because this widow bothers me, I will give her legal protection, otherwise by continually coming she will wear me out.'" And the Lord said, "Hear what the unrighteous judge said; now, will not God bring about justice for His elect who cry to Him day and night, and will He delay long over them? I tell you that He will bring about justice for them quickly. However, when the Son of Man comes, will He find faith on the earth?"

Luke 18:1-8 NASB 1995

Earnest persistence in prayer is a kind of sanctified rebellion against the status quo of a society that is not interested in the kingdom of God, but rather caught up in its societal point system.[4] Earnest prayer refuses to give in to the status quo: the injustice, the sin, the idolatry and the evil that threatens to overwhelm us. Earnest prayer insists on the full coming of the kingdom because there is nothing better.

Why do we need to insist and persist in prayer? Why should we pray earnestly? Here are four related reasons:

1. Because the Lord tells us to. This is how he brings about the fullness of his kingdom—through the earnest prayers of his people who do not give up. This is part of our role as kingdom agents.

2. The enemy, though defeated, still makes war against us. The situation is deadly serious.

3. The Father wants us to be more fully aware of what we are asking for and its implications. Are we asking for his kingdom to come or ours? Just how badly do we want his kingdom to come?

4. The Father usually answers the prayers of his people *through* his people. That's why the answer to our prayers is the Holy Spirit[5]. Are we serious enough about what we're asking for to get involved? Are we willing to take the time? The resources? To undergo more training from the hand of the Lord? To have our typical ways of thinking challenged? Or are we looking for God to do things for us without our involvement? Are we looking for some magic pill? Since God uses his people to answer prayer, we should persist in prayer because sometimes they aren't ready yet to be the means through which God answers.

It's been said, "If you ask for more patience or love or growth, the Lord will give you a challenging problem so you learn patience or love as you learn to trust him." And who wants a challenging problem? The truth of this statement highlights one of the reasons we are reluctant to really want the kingdom to come in our own lives. Wanting the kingdom, asking, seeking, knocking, persisting, and insisting that God fulfill his promises—all these things could very easily upset our lives, reorder our priorities and make life quite inconvenient and challenging.

Many years ago, we were packing up our belongings as we prepared to return from Chile to the States to visit our supporting churches for a year. The worst storm in recent memory hit us just as we were packing up. We already had our tickets and it looked like it was going to be a huge challenge to leave on time. On top of all that, we needed to sell our car in order to be able to purchase a vehicle to use in the States. But just a few days before we had to leave, the engine developed a serious problem. I was feeling overwhelmed. If we postponed our departure, we would have to pay a penalty, and money was short. In the midst of all this, I remember thinking, "Maybe the Lord is giving us the opportunity to learn to trust him more." Then I thought, "Lord, I'd be glad to learn that lesson, but couldn't it be later on when we're more settled? Right now, I've got to get us home!" Later I realized just how ridiculous my thoughts were.

Christians are not called to be masochists. We are not called to love pain. But we are called to a glorious kingdom that can be had only as we are willing to let go of all else. We pray earnestly as we are willing to give up all for the sake of the kingdom.

Looking to Jesus

It's not that God wants us to beg, as if he weren't willing to help or wanted to make us suffer wondering whether he cared enough or had enough power. After all, when we ask him to bring in the fullness of the kingdom, we're asking him to do what he's already promised to do.

> Do not be afraid, little flock, for your Father has chosen gladly to give you the kingdom.
> Luke 12:32 NASB 1995

In fact, he *has* given us the kingdom by sending Jesus. Jesus is the proof that the heavenly Father is ready and willing to give us what we need for the progress of the kingdom. Jesus' death, resurrection ascension and outpouring of the Holy Spirit are proof that the Father is pleased to give us the kingdom.

Jesus reveals the extent of this willingness by comparing and contrasting the heavenly Father with an earthly father. I know that my earthly father would bend over backwards to help me with my needs. So, think about your earthly father, however imperfect he may be, and then contemplate this: the heavenly Father is much more ready and willing than even the most loving earthly father to answer our prayers for the coming of the kingdom.

> Now suppose one of you fathers is asked by his son for a fish; he will not give him a snake instead of a fish, will he? Or if he is asked for an egg, he will not give him a scorpion, will he? If you then, being evil, know how to give good gifts to your children, how much more will your heavenly Father give the Holy Spirit to those who ask Him?"
>
> Luke 11:11-13 NASB 1995

If the unjust judge finally answered the request of the widow just to keep her from bothering him, how much more will the heavenly Father who is the *just* judge give us what we request if we pray without giving up and without giving in to the status quo!

> now, will not God bring about justice for His elect who cry to Him day and night, and will He delay long over them?
>
> Luke 18:7 NASB 1995

James gives the example of Elijah as someone who prayed earnestly.

> Therefore... pray for one another so that you may be healed. The effective prayer of a righteous man can accomplish much. Elijah was a man with a nature like ours, and he prayed earnestly that it would not rain, and it did not rain on the earth for three years and six months. Then he prayed again, and the sky poured rain and the earth produced its fruit.

James 5:16-18 NASB 1995

Even though we might tend to idealize Elijah, James emphasizes the point that he was a man like us: with the fears, doubts and failings that we also experience.[6] In the context, praying earnestly is something that any forgiven person can do. When you pray with a good conscience, having confessed your sins, your prayers are effective.

What is required is not some super spirituality. What is required is faith that looks away from self to the Savior. The author of Hebrews puts it this way:

> And without faith it is impossible to please Him, for he who comes to God must believe that He is and that He is a rewarder of those who seek Him.
>
> Hebrews 11:6 NASB 1995

Now that Christ has brought the kingdom, faith in God implies faith in Christ. Earnestness in prayer is not a matter of mustering any strength we might have in ourselves. To "earnestly seek him" is nothing more than to look away increasingly from self to Christ and his righteousness, to the promises of God in Christ that he will bring us into the fullness of the kingdom. The problem is that it's very easy to start looking to ourselves instead of looking to Christ in faith, especially in the face of challenges that loom like immovable mountains. The flesh tempts us to give up. The culture around us tempts us to give in to the status quo and its societal point system. As we begin to look to ourselves, as we begin to give in to the status quo of our culture, our sense of urgency, earnestness and fervency dissipates. We settle for less. We lose sight of the inestimable value of the kingdom.

When you are tempted to give up in prayer, look away from yourself and look to Christ—what he has done and what he promises to do. When you are discouraged, stop focusing on yourself and your challenging situation. Look away from yourself and from the cultural expectations that force themselves upon you as urgently important. Rather, look to Christ. Then view the situation you are experiencing in light of who he is and what he has promised to do. When you are tempted to sin, look away from yourself and the cultural expectations that bombard you every day. Rather, look to Christ. When you are wondering if you are really a Christian, stop focusing on yourself and the cultural expectations that tell you what to believe and what not to believe. Rather, look to Christ. Remind yourself of who he is, what he has done, and what he promises to do. Earnestness in prayer grows— not as we try really hard in our own strength. Rather, earnestness in prayer grows as we look away from ourselves and our circumstances as the measure of who we are and who we want to become, and as we look to Christ and the reality of the kingdom into which he has brought us.

The Lord asks us to be willing to give up all for the sake of the kingdom. The question is, how badly do we want the fullness of the kingdom to come? How much do we trust Christ to take care of us if we are called to give up something for the sake of the kingdom? We must pray earnestly because the kingdom is worth more than anything else.

Follow-up

1. Would you say that you pray earnestly? Give examples.
2. How does double-mindedness affect your prayer life? Give examples.
3. If someone were to follow you around for a week, what would they say about the level of your desire for the kingdom to come in its fullness? What would be their evidence? How do you feel about this?

4. How much time do you spend in prayer each day or each week? Are you happy with this amount of time? If not, what are you going to do about it?

5. Are you hesitant to ask the Lord for greater growth—like more patience, or more love? If your answer is yes, why do you think that is? If not, share with someone a time you did this and what happened as a result.

6. How well have you developed the ability to look away from yourself to Christ in the face of temptation to sin or to give up? Give examples.

Chapter 9

Pray in Ministry

When I opened the church door that morning, the three young men I had invited to join me in a discipleship program had already arrived—very excited about the two hours we were about to spend together in prayer. This prayer time seemed to go by very quickly. It was an exciting time that we all looked forward to. Why was it so exciting? Because we were praying in the context of being together on a mission—of being engaged together in ministry—and that made all the difference.

Prayer is much more effective when carried out in the context of using your gifts in ministry. The style of leadership I typically see in churches, however, is not designed to get believers involved in ministry. Typical church leadership can be summed up this way:

> "As your God-ordained leader I'm here to provide an authoritative interpretation of Scripture, administer the sacraments and exercise church discipline when someone falls grievously into sin. I'm here to help you be a better Christian and have a meaningful church experience."

Sometimes this involves the elder leading an "under shepherd group," or leading a Bible study. However, these are typically affected negatively by a reductionistic view of discipleship that over focuses on the transmission of information. In any case, whatever the stated goal of leadership, the goal-in-use is typically individualistic and designed simply to satisfy the spiritual needs of the individual. With this kind of leadership, the church becomes merely a provider of spiritual goods and services.

Many churches go one of two ways when it comes to leadership: (1) pressuring people to get involved in programs to such an extent that they get burned out, or (2) telling people, "If you have a problem let me know. Otherwise I'll leave you alone." Ephesians 4 says the job of leaders is to "equip" the saints so they can do ministry. In the Greek, the word translated "equip" means "to make complete." It involves more than just teaching classes or otherwise passing along information. Leadership means explicitly pointing people to Christ, to his great promises, to the great adventure and mission to which he has called us. It involves modeling ministry, watching people do ministry and giving them feedback, and getting involved with people. It involves investing in people—making disciples—rather than either pressuring them or leaving them alone. Why are there so few elders who really believe–and put into practice–Ephesians 4?

Following is what I believe to be a more biblical goal of church leadership:

"You, the members of this church are God's kingdom agents–the ones through whom he largely fulfills his promise to bring his kingdom to bear on planet earth. We need your gifts and we need you to be able to use your gifts synergistically with the other members of the church–and even with other churches–so that God's kingdom is increasingly brought to bear on our culture in our city through our unified godly influence. Our job as leaders is to exercise the kind of influence that will make that goal an increasing reality–even as we continue to walk the way of the cross."

This second expression reveals a kind of leadership that is much more missional than the first. Instead of leaders trying to provide spiritual goods and services for spiritual consumers, they promote a synergistic engagement as kingdom agents in the mission to which God has called his church. I'm not suggesting some kind of triumphalist grab for political power on the part of the church. I'm saying we need to do a better job of training people to use the ordinary means of grace to bring God's kingdom to bear in the places we live. It seems clear to me that the recent open raging of the evil one–along with the obvious advance of evil agendas in our country–point to the fact that the church has not been functioning adequately as the salt and light our King intended us to be.

The task of church leaders is to help the church as a whole be involved in ministry. Yet many Christians participate in worship services and even in prayer meetings without using their gifts to advance the mission of the church by being involved in ministry. In this chapter we will see that prayer is much more meaningful and powerful when carried out in the context of the God-given ministry of the church, and in line with the specific way your own church carries out that ministry.

Prayer and the Ministry of the Church

The New Testament identifies six aspects of the ministry of the church. These are as follows: proclamation of the good news of the kingdom, diaconal service to those in need, fellowship among God's people, teaching God's Word, and worshipping God. Figure 8 illustrates the fact that prayer should be carried out in the context of these other aspects of the ministry of the church.[1]

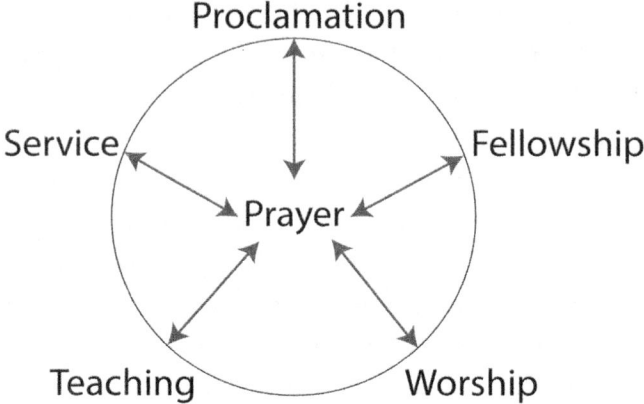

Figure 8. Prayer should influence and be influenced by the
other aspects of ministry

Prayer that is divorced from the action and the relationships
involved in these aspects of the ministry of the church quickly
becomes a boring chore. Jesus didn't pray for the sake of carrying out
a religious ritual. His prayers were connected to his ministry. For
example, before choosing the twelve disciples, he spent all night in
prayer.[2] Prayer is much more meaningful and effective when it is
done in the context of ministry.

More specifically, prayer should be carried out in the context of
the other five aspects of ministry because they are designed to enrich
each other and to propel each other forward in the mission. Table
1 provides some examples of how prayer can be positively enriched
by the other ministry systems.

A	B
Ministry	**Enrichment of Prayer by this Ministry**
Worship	Motive for prayer is a response to the glory of God in Christ.
Teaching	Reasons for requests are based on God's promises, actions, and character, and are enriched by the experience of having acted in faith based on these.
Proclamation	Prayer controlled by the good news of the coming of the kingdom in Christ. Enriched by the experience of having engaged people with the good news.
Fellowship	All aspects of prayer are enriched by the contributions of other believers. Fellowship provides a wider and deeper perspective on what to pray for and how to pray.
Service	Prayer is enriched by the experience of serving others in their need.

Table 1. Enrichment of Prayer by Ministries of the Church

When prayer is not influenced by these other areas of ministry, it becomes distorted. For example, worshipping God reminds us that our prayers should not be me-and-mine-centered. We pray, for example, that God's name will be recognized as holy—set apart from all other names and worshipped. So when we ask for something for ourselves and our loved ones, we do so in the context of worshipping God and not merely for our comfort.

When prayer does not flow out of sound Biblical teaching including the proclamation of the good news of the kingdom, the stated or unstated reasons for praying about something tend to be based on personal and cultural priorities. For example, when I hear someone asking God to heal a person who is sick, I often wonder *why* they are making this request since most of the time no reasons are given. I typically don't hear something like the following: "Lord, please heal Mrs. Jones because she is your child and your Word says you have compassion on your children." When time after time no reasons are given, I begin to wonder if the person praying has fallen into the circumstantial perspective—assuming[3] that the great divide in life is not between the Kingdom of God and the domain of darkness but between good circumstances and bad circumstances. Relating our prayers to the truths of God's Word—and in particular to the good news of the kingdom of God—enables us to have proper reasons for our requests.

Without the influence of Biblical fellowship, prayer can easily become an individualistic focus on me-and-mine.[4] On the other hand, true Biblical fellowship also protects us from the tendency to use corporate prayer as an excuse for gossip, complaining and venting (usually in a very polite and discreet way.) It also protects us from praying as cliques. In addition, fellowship provides a wider and deeper perspective on how to pray for a given situation.[5]

Finally, prayer is enriched by the experience of using your gifts to serve others in their need. Such service allows us to see more clearly and deeply the needs of others, and develops in us genuine concern for others.

Of course, people are gifted in different areas. Not everyone will be involved equally in every area of ministry. My point is that prayer should not be isolated from the ministry of the church. The prayers of the church are enriched as they are carried out in the context of the other five aspects of ministry.

Prayer and the Ministry of Your Church

Furthermore, prayer should not be isolated from the *specific way* your local church has decided to carry out its ministry. I will examine this from four related perspectives: 1) the need for ministry priorities, 2) avoiding the pitfalls related to the ministry priorities of your local church, 3) praying in line with your church's mission and 4) praying for cross-cultural missionaries.

The Need for Priorities in Ministry

It is impossible not to have priorities when it comes to the six aspects of ministry because, unlike God, we can't do everything at once. God designed us in a way that we have to lead out with some good things over other good things.[6] For example, some churches lead out with teaching. Others lead out with fellowship. Others give a certain priority to worship. Of course, none of the six aspects of ministry should be left out. But there is a sense in which these six aspects are not completely different from each other. If you dig down deep enough into fellowship, for example, you will find teaching. True fellowship involves admonishing one another with the truth. If you dig down deep enough into teaching, you will find service because the truth pushes us out to serve. So, yes, a church should do all of these. But they are best accomplished by leading out with one or two and doing the others through these that are given a certain priority.

In other words, prayer should arise out of what is often referred to as the church's *philosophy of ministry*. A philosophy of ministry is a church's system of priorities in ministry. Of all the good and Biblical things the church could do, what things does it tend to do first? What do visitors see first when they walk in the door? What are its ministry priorities?

How should a church decide on its priorities? As Figure 9 suggests, a philosophy of ministry—with its priorities—might be thought of as (1) the application of God's Word (2) by a group of people with certain gifts (3) doing ministry in a particular context.[7]

Figure 9. Philosophy of Ministry Elements

A church's decisions about these philosophy of ministry issues will affect how they pray. Of all the good things you could pray about —and it would be impossible to pray specifically about everything— what will you focus on? A church's philosophy of ministry will affect its priorities in prayer.

Avoiding Priority Pitfalls

As a church formulates and carries out its ministry, there are two tempting errors it must avoid if it is to be effective. The first error involves an overemphasis on the context and its needs. In this case the church decides its priorities primarily on the basis of what the people who live in the area want; and what they want—their felt needs—typically have nothing to do with the kingdom of God affecting their lives. This would be what some people call a "seeker-driven"[8] church. A church like this loses its Biblical bearings and is unable to minister effectively. It becomes a club of the community. Prayer—along with the other aspects of ministry—is distorted and loses its kingdom perspective by over focusing on meeting the felt needs of the community/context. Instead of praying about the coming of the kingdom into the lives of those who live in the community/context, prayer becomes more about connecting with the felt needs of the community with the intention of getting more people to come to church. For example, a typical prayer in this scenario might be, "Lord, help our worship team to be full of the Spirit (read "attractive" or even "entertaining") so more people will be attracted to our service."

On the other hand, if church priorities are determined primarily by the gifts of the church without considering the needs of the community from a Biblical point of view, then the church becomes ingrown: a club for people who like good teaching, or a club for people who like fellowship among themselves. Prayer—along with the other aspects of ministry—is thus distorted and becomes ingrown and church-centered. In this scenario there is little prayer for the conversion and spiritual growth of people who live in the community surrounding the church. The focus tends to be on church members— their health, their well-being, and maybe even their spiritual growth.

A third pitfall when it comes to ministry priorities is simply not thinking things through. Even if your church is able to avoid praying within a seeker-driven or ingrown paradigm, sometimes churches simply don't have an *intentional* philosophy of ministry that focuses their prayers in a specific way. It could be that your church has simply fallen into a set of priorities without giving it much thought. In this case it's likely that your church is not aware of its priorities.

This lack of thinking things through has an impact on the prayers of the church. Let me give an example. Let's say you are in a prayer meeting, and everyone asks for prayer for some relative who lives in another state and that no one has ever met before. It's fine and proper, of course, to support a fellow believer in prayer for some relative who lives far away. It's also good to pray for cross-cultural missionaries and for the church in other countries. But if there is no intentionality about connecting prayer to the specific mission of your particular church, then you're going to be missing out on an important dimension of prayer. If prayers are *primarily* haphazard requests of isolated individuals who happen to attend the same church, but who are not engaged together in a mission with a focused expression of love for the King and his kingdom contextualized to a particular shared place in the world, prayer will be less interesting, less satisfying, and less effective.

Many churches actually have a mission statement, and maybe even a plan for carrying it out. However, putting one's theoretical priorities on paper doesn't mean that the actions of the church are actually in line with what is written. We should distinguish between a church's *espoused* philosophy of ministry, and its philosophy of ministry *in-use*. To get at the philosophy of ministry that is actually being used would require analyzing things like what decisions are made, how and why they are made, how the church uses its resources, how leaders relate to the congregation, how members relate to each other, and so on. In other words, we would have to discern the real priorities of the church by examining its actions or lack of actions.

Ask yourself these questions: Do I know what the ministry priorities of my church are? Do those priorities fit the gifts of the church? Are they being effectively leveraged to reach out to the community surrounding the church? How does this set of priorities direct the prayers of the church in the direction of fulfilling its mission in the community as well as in the world?

Praying in Line with Your Church's Mission

It is much better, of course, to have an intentional philosophy of ministry—to know *why* you have certain emphases and to have good and Biblical and contextual reasons for them—than simply to fall into routine patterns that end up being your philosophy of ministry by default and that may or may not be effective.

Imagine how ineffective it would be for a battalion of soldiers to go into battle with no clear and unified set of priorities. The prayers of a church without a clear philosophy of ministry are like such a battalion. The prayers of church members should flow from a keen awareness of its primary objective, the characteristics of the situation on the ground, and how to leverage its strengths in that situation. I'm concerned that prayer in many churches is disconnected from a keen sense of "we are on a mission here in our part of the world, I know what our mission is, and this is my part in it."

Many churches in the United States don't view themselves as on a mission. They reserve that word for cross-cultural missionaries. In my circles they use the word "missions." I prefer to talk about "the mission of the church." Whether that mission is "here" or "there" is not irrelevant but is of secondary importance. As mentioned in chapter 3, all believers are to be on a mission.

Within this "missions" mentality there is something very exciting about going on a "missions trip"—or being a full-time missionary, for that matter—an excitement that is not usually associated with evangelizing one's neighbor or colleague at work. In fact, there are many people who have gone on "missions trips" without ever having attempted to evangelize a neighbor or a colleague at work. So why do we make this distinction and why do we reach out so little to those of our own culture? I think we don't reach out to people within our own culture because we've become so much like the surrounding culture that we don't have a compelling message that will reach into their hearts with kingdom life and joy.

Whatever the reason for downplaying the local mission of the church, the members and leaders of a particular church should view themselves as a team put together by the Lord himself and assigned a particular mission: that of advancing the kingdom—the reign of Jesus over the people in the area in which they have been placed.[9] Prayer takes on much greater significance when viewed as a critical resource of a team called to carry out a kingdom mission within the area of the world where the Lord has providentially placed them. People who know best how to pray are typically those who are experienced in spiritual warfare on behalf of the King and the kingdom in their particular area of the world. They know the strengths of their church, they know and have a love for their context, and want to see it transformed by the power of the gospel.

In our first church plant in Chile, we ended up carrying out the ministry by giving priority to fellowship and service. These were the areas to which the people in the context were more responsive. It was a poor area of town and there were a lot of material needs. Furthermore, the Chilean culture gives a strong priority to relationships. It was not easy for us to come to this conclusion since my strongest gifts were in the areas of teaching and proclamation. But we found ways to teach, proclaim the kingdom, pray and worship by giving priority to fellowship and service. Here are some examples:

1. As the pastor, I visited people a lot. This was not my strong suit and people didn't open up to me right away. But I found that by visiting people, issues would come up and I was able to apply God's Word and the good news of the kingdom to their problems. Furthermore, I grew as I worked at applying God's Word through avenues of fellowship and service.

2. Most people who lived in the area where we planted the church didn't have a vehicle. So it was difficult for them to go grocery shopping downtown where they could purchase things more cheaply. There was only so much they could carry home with them on the bus. They typically purchased food at local markets where the prices were much higher. As a result of this problem, we decided to form a coop. We would purchase some grocery items in bulk at lower prices, and then sell them to people of the church at cost.

3. Most people who lived in our part of town didn't have good health insurance. Typically they would take a bus to the clinic, where—unless they were dying—they would get some pain pills and told to go home. Sometimes it wasn't worth going when it was cold out because they would get sicker just standing in line. Since I had a car, people would often ask me to take them to the clinic. As I carried out this task, I learned how unhelpful—and sometimes even harmful—going to the clinic was. As I prayed about what to do, the Lord brought James 5:14-15 to mind. "Dare I take this seriously?" I asked myself. The meaning of the words was unmistakable. So I decided to take God at his word. I talked to the session of the church

and we decided to pray for the sick every Sunday during the worship service. Not everyone was healed when we prayed,[10] but the Lord did indeed heal people regularly through this ministry. Twice the Lord brought back to health someone the doctors said was about to die. By serving the people in this way, we all learned more about taking God as his word, trusting him, and taking steps of faith.

4. When I invited several young men to join me in ministry, I did not set up the program as a typical school. There was a focus on our relationship as a group of believers going on a mission together. Yes, part of the time was spent studying books. But the highlight for them—and the main reason they were interested—was the fellowship we experienced as a band of brothers involved together in an important mission. These Chilean men with whom I prayed for two hours a day came to be excited about prayer because we were engaged in action and relationship together. The night before, we had all been out evangelizing, discipling, using our gifts to serve those in need, or worshipping God and having fellowship in a home meeting. We had seen the huge challenges before us. We had seen the Lord at work. When we met for prayer in the morning it was in the context of our ministry together the night before. When we studied theology, it was in the hope of preparing better for our mission together the next evening.

5. We organized a Vacation Bible School during their break from school. This was something most people in the area had never seen before. Many mothers saw this as a service provided by the church—something for their children to do during the school break. We organized the VBS not around communicating content—although we certainly did that. The focus was on relationships with

the children. Eventually there were 250 children who attended the program. The enthusiasm of the children for the program opened doors for us as we later visited the parents. Many of these parents eventually started attending our church.

6. As many of the members of the church got involved in these activities—and others at least saw what was happening in terms of ministry—their prayers were focused on the fulfillment of the specific mission of the local church.

Praying for Cross-cultural Missionaries

Part of the ministry of a local church is being involved with cross-cultural missionaries who minister in other parts of the world. As we have noted previously, this should not be done as an *alternative* to being themselves on a mission in their particular area of the world. Rather, in addition to being a means of involvement in the mission of the church worldwide, it's a way for the local church to avoid local-centrism.[11]

It's very easy for a local church to become unaware of its own tendencies to idolatry. It can become so influenced by the surrounding culture that it ends up being unable to have a significant mission to that culture. It seems to me, for example, that the values of comfort and ease that our culture holds have infiltrated the church to such an extent that the church has a hard time seeing itself as being on a mission. If churches do reach out, their message often comes across as "Christ can give you comfort and ease better than anything else you might try."

An almost completely overlooked value of being involved with cross-cultural missionaries is the ability it gives you as a sending/supporting church to see yourself from the point of view of a church in a different part of the world. What can you learn from them about your own mission and the ways you are carrying it out? How can interaction with them—probably through the missionary you support—help you avoid idolatries in your own ministry? This stance and view of mission would require much humility and effort. But I think it's imperative that churches take this stance.

Taking this perspective would necessarily change the way your church prays for cross-cultural missionaries. Instead of merely praying for the success of their mission, you would also pray that the missionary would learn important things that will in turn be helpful to you. The annual mission conference would be less about inspiring you with glowing reports than about helping you be more effective in your own local mission.

Following are some suggestions about praying for cross-cultural missionaries your church supports:

1. Designate a group of people to interact with a specific supported missionary. This group should communicate with the rest of the church—especially the church leadership.

2. Find out from the missionary the particular issues he faces. How are these similar or different from the issues typically faced by churches in the United States? What truths of the Bible do these issues bring to the forefront?

3. Pray for the missionary as he faces these issues.

4. Every time the missionary sends a letter, someone from the group should respond. This response should be more than a mere acknowledgement of receipt, but should involve a learning attitude. Ask questions that might eventually help your local church carry out its mission more effectively. This will enrich your prayer and extend it to involve your own local mission.

5. Set up your annual mission conference to be more than an inspiration to giving and praying for the congregation. Set it up to be a learning event that equips your people to be more effective in their own mission. Don't limit the supported missionary to a mere report. Encourage him to

share from God's Word what he has learned about God, about himself, and about the mission of the church by ministering in a different culture. Prayers at the annual mission conference should reflect this attitude.

Praying for cross-cultural missionaries certainly includes asking the Lord to give them strength and success in their mission. But it also includes asking the Lord to teach them important things you need to learn for your own local mission.

Prayer is much more exciting and effective when people know what the specific mission of their church is and are involved in it. When people are aware of their particular gifts as a church, of how these gifts can be used to reach out to their particular context and of how gifts and context come together effectively through guidance from the Word, prayer becomes an integral part of your church's specific mission instead of an isolated event.

Follow-up

1. What are the particular gifts and emphases of your church as you consider the six aspects of the ministry of the church? Give evidence for your answer.
2. What are the particular needs of the context in which your church exists?
3. Does prayer seem isolated from the ministry of the church, or do you feel it is an integral part of who you are and what you are doing as a church member? Explain your answer and give evidence.
4. How do you feel when you hear someone pray in awe of Jesus the King, and with a clear longing for his kingdom

to come? Can you specify why it makes you feel the way it does?

5. Does your church have a written mission statement? What evidence is there that your church is making progress on fulfilling its mission?

6. Does your church have a written philosophy of ministry? If not, does it have a set of priorities? What are they?

7. Do you think the ministry priorities of your church fit with its gifts?

8. Do you think the ministry priorities of your church fit with the needs of the context?

9. Do you sense that prayers in your church are primarily random requests arising from individuals who happen to attend the same church, or do they dovetail with the specific mission of the church, its giftedness and the needs of the context? Give examples.

Chapter 10

Pray Together

Having attended many church prayer meetings and and small group meetings, I have gotten the impression that—at least in my circles—Christians don't really like praying together. If there were greater interest, there would be more people attending prayer meetings. Furthermore, most prayer meetings are more about Bible study than about prayer—which often takes up a small percentage of the time set aside for the "prayer meeting."

The Power of Corporate Prayer

Is there any benefit for God's people to pray together, or is it just as good for all of them to pray individually? I believe that both should be done. In this section I would like to make the case for the importance of corporate prayer, which has to do with the intersection of prayer and fellowship. When you consider the power associated with the synergy of God's people (see below), and apply it to prayer, the conclusion is that corporate prayer has a very important role in God's kingdom purposes. This seems to be the intent of these verses:

Again I say to you, that if two of you agree on earth about anything that they may ask, it shall be done for them by My Father who is in heaven. For where two or three have gathered together in My name, I am there in their midst.

Matthew 18:19-20 NASB 1995

In the context, Jesus is talking about agreeing about what to do with someone in the church who needs discipline. But it seems to me that verses 19-20 express a general principle that has wider application than just the issue of discipline. The words "anything you ask" seem to refer to prayer in a way that goes beyond the issue of discipline.[1] Furthermore, verse 20 has the ring of a general principle. God is with all his people through the Spirit, whether they are alone or with other believers. But there seems to be something special about God's presence when at least 2 are gathered together in his name to agree about what they are asking for in prayer.

God says of the people at Babel, "If as one people speaking the same language they have begun to do this, then nothing they plan to do will be impossible for them."[2] God is making the point that there is special power present when people are united behind a cause. There is power in synergy--whether for good or for evil. In Genesis 11, God frustrated the formation of an evil synergy by confusing their language, and in Genesis 12 he began his plan to form a much more powerful synergy for good: a people for whom nothing would be impossible. We see this power foreshadowed in God's ability to do the impossible through the marriage relationship of Abraham and Sarah. It is fulfilled in Christ who, having defeated death, has all power and authority and who, on the day of Pentecost, poured out the gift of the eschatological Spirit[3] on his people. On that day, people from every nation under heaven heard this good news in their own languages. Both at Babel and at Pentecost there is a miracle of languages. In the former case to frustrate an evil synergy, and in the latter case to create a more powerful synergy for bringing in the fullness of God's kingdom.

Church fellowship—designed to be a powerful way to advance the kingdom—in my context has often been reduced to having coffee and donuts between Sunday school and the worship service or to a Wednesday evening meal together. George and Amanda[4] had recently moved into town and began attending a new church. They decided to participate in the Wednesday evening meal, but no one came to sit by them. Eventually they—the new people—had to take the initiative to get to know those who had been attending for years. Edward and Sheryl[5] experienced something similar. They began attending a new church and looked for opportunities to join a small group. But no one invited them to join, and when they did try to join they were told the group was full. They had to wait for some new people to join the church and formed a small group with them. Church cliques weaken what is meant to be a powerful synergistic fellowship of God's people.

The spiritual warfare to which the apostle Paul calls us and in which prayer figures so prominently has collective as well as individual implications. In our English translation, the "you," that is implicit in the verbs of Ephesians 6:10-20 is plural in the Greek original. As in any kind of warfare, the members of God's army must have each other's back. In my church planting experience, when someone was converted, we found that within about two weeks they would experience a harsh attack from the evil one. We also found that if the body of Christ rallied around them with prayer and using their gifts to be supportive, the new convert continued on as a member of the body. If we failed as a body to rally around, we found that the new convert would fall away.

The evil one would like nothing better than for believers to take off their armor and put down their sword and shield. Let's encourage each other so that we will be able to stand our ground in the evil day. Rally around those who are discouraged, weak or sidetracked for whatever reason. Sometimes they need us to attend to their wounds. Other times they need to be admonished. Sometimes they need to be forgiven.[6] The remedy for a disabled, weakened or discouraged soldier should fit the situation. In any case, we need each other. One less fighting soldier puts us all in greater danger.

Based on the preceding we conclude that there is power in corporate prayer. So, when after Pentecost God's people were threatened by the local leaders, they got together to pray:

> When they had been released, they went to their own companions and reported all that the chief priests and the elders had said to them. And when they heard this, they lifted their voices to God with one accord....
>
> Acts 4:23-24 NASB 1995

In response to their prayer, God answered this way:

> And when they had prayed, the place where they had gathered together was shaken, and they were all filled with the Holy Spirit and began to speak the word of God with boldness.
>
> Acts 4:31 NASB 1995

In the middle of the 18th century Jonathan Edwards, focusing his argument on Zechariah 8:20-22[7] and supporting a call to prayer that came from the church in Scotland in 1744, argued that God would bring about great revival and growth in his church in response to God's people from all over the world forming a visible union and agreeing to pray for it.[8] Edwards' proposal included people getting together for prayer with neighbors where possible. While people who live in different countries can't always get together in one place to pray, they can agree to pray for the same things.[9]

Learning through Prayer

I have found myself increasingly agreeing with Edwards on this point as I have reflected on my many years of cross-cultural mission experience. I've often wondered if one of the reasons the church has decreased in number and power in different places around the world might be due to the limitations created by the blindness of cultural idolatry that could be addressed by praying together in the ways I've described. Let me elaborate a little.

When Paul talks about being able to understand what is beyond understanding "together with all the saints,"[10] I believe he means that the members of the body of Christ need each other in order to understand what is otherwise beyond understanding.[11] Every culture's understanding of the Bible is conditioned to some extent by its own cultural assumptions. This is both helpful and a detriment. It is helpful because every culture reflects God's glory in special ways. So, the church in every culture has insights into the meaning of God's Word that tend to be less obvious to other cultures.[12] Fellowship and prayer across cultures thus helps us get a broader and deeper view of who God is and what he has done. We need each other to gain a fuller understanding of God's Word.

On the other hand, a culturally conditioned understanding of the Bible is detrimental because of the fall. Sin encourages us to over depend on our unique perspective on God's Word--as if it were the only one.[13] We confuse the message of the gospel with our culturally conditioned understanding of it. This makes the process of learning from the church in other cultures particularly challenging. It requires the power of the Holy Spirit.

In many cases, the problem is not that missionaries or local leaders are not loving. Very often they love each other--but only to the extent of their self-awareness. That is, lack of cultural self-awareness limits their ability to love because it limits their knowledge--of themselves, of the situation, of the local leaders, and even of the Word of God.

As an example, let's look at the case of a group of US missionaries who were working with some Latin American leaders to plant a church in Latin America. All of these workers loved each other and got along well. But none of them liked the weekly prayer and planning meeting. They thought it was sluggish and boring.

The US leader of the team planned and led the meeting and tried to make it as efficient as possible. That way they weren't wasting time and had more time for informal fellowship afterwards. The missionary assumption was that efficiency leads to effectiveness and also allows more time for fellowship.

The Latin Americans, on the other hand, felt that the goal orientation of the meeting limited "relational talk," which made the meeting shallow and uninteresting to them. Relational talk included the following: (a) sharing informally how things were going in the various ministry responsibilities of each person; (b) informal talk unrelated to the agenda of the meeting that promoted camaraderie; (c) talk—even jokes—that promoted a relaxed atmosphere conducive to sharing important things; (d) spontaneous prayer; (e) the expression of emotions; and (f) background or tangential comments.

The US missionaries said it would not be helpful to include relational talk in the meeting. In their minds, this should be done after the meeting is over in an informal atmosphere. They were frustrated by the tendency of people to have private conversations and to tell jokes during the meeting, which got the discussion off topic. Furthermore, they didn't think the meeting was the appropriate place for emotional expression.

The Latin Americans, on the other hand, said that if the meeting were to be effective these excluded forms of talk must be included as part of the meeting and not just allowed in the informal time that followed the meeting. They insisted that from a Latin American point of view, it was the only way to motivate people to participate, and to create a relaxed atmosphere in which they felt comfortable enough to say what they really thought about things. The Latin American assumption was that fellowship incorporated into the meeting leads to effectiveness. It's the best way to get people to participate fully in the meeting.

So, the US missionaries gave priority to efficiency in the meeting in order to have time afterwards for fellowship. The Latin American leaders gave priority to fellowship as the means to be effective in ministry. The lack of awareness of these hidden assumptions made their prayer and planning meetings less effective than they could have been. We need to find better ways to engage each other to overcome the tendency to interpret others primarily through the grid of one's own culture.

So, when Paul talks in Ephesians 3:10 about the multicultural church reflecting the multifaceted wisdom of God and thus teaching the angels[14] more of the depths of that wisdom, this is one of his implications: We will not see the power of the gospel unleashed as it could be in a given area until we learn just how much we have been affected by our own culture. We need to increasingly see how our culture has sharpened our view of some things and distorted our view of others. And we learn this primarily as we relate to people—especially Christians—from other cultures.[15]

Being a cross-cultural missionary can provide just this opportunity: for both cultures involved to learn about themselves, to get out of their cultural idolatries (held culturally in place by demonic forces), and to create kingdom synergy. Churches should invite missionaries to speak, not only to hear reports on how the Lord is at work in faraway places, but also to find out what the cross-cultural missionaries have learned about our own culture—both its special reflections of God's glory and its blind spots.

Talking to a missionary is not the only way to become culturally self-aware. In a globalized world you don't need to travel across the seas to have this kind of experience. It has come to our doorstep. Even reading books by Christians in other places and other times can be helpful in overcoming the limitations of cultural bias.[16]

So, partnership in the gospel across cultures should not be viewed as a nice but unnecessary step for mature churches to take. Rather, it is of the essence of the gospel ministry. Normally it's only as we get together, really understanding each other in love, that the power of the gospel is unleashed.[17] The increasing interaction of Christians from different cultures in our time is, I believe, one way God is overcoming this ethnocentric blindness that has hindered the growth of the church. But we need to take advantage of this movement by viewing such interaction as an opportunity to learn from each other about the greatness of God's glory in Christ. One of the ways this can happen is by talking together about what is important to pray about, and then praying together. To do this well can be difficult. But it is worth the effort.

A similar limitation can occur when people from the same culture fail to learn about God through interaction with people who have different personality types and background experiences. This is one of the hard and wonderful lessons I learned by spending so much time living and ministering in Chile. As it turns out, my personality type is the exact opposite of what the Chilean culture appreciates and expects of people. Ministering in Chile under those conditions was very challenging and, in some ways, painful to me. At one point it eventually got back to me that people in the church didn't have "confianza" with me. It took me a while to figure out even what that meant. It's not that they didn't trust and respect me. It was more like they didn't feel they had permission to speak freely in my presence. I guess you could say their respect for me was great, but their sense of freedom was small.

Looking back, I would say the Lord sent me to Chile not only to plant churches, but also to help me grow through contact with people —especially Christians—who are very different from me. It was one of the most beneficial experiences of my life because I learned so much about myself, my culture, and about God. Although I've grown a lot in this area, it's something I still struggle with. My personality type tends to project an air of confidence that often—contrary to my desires—shuts down conversation. I guess you could say there is a legitimate reflection of God's glory there, but shutting down conversation is a distortion due to the effects of sin.

When we hold believers who are different at arm's length, and thus inhibit learning from them, we do ourselves and the church a disservice. Maybe it's the person who rubs you the wrong way that you need most in order to grow. Talking together about our prayer concerns is not easy, but it can help us focus these requests in a more Christ-centered way so we can pray more intelligently and effectively.

Corporate prayer helps us overcome the hidden (even to ourselves) self-centeredness and ethnocentricity of our prayers. It also brings our different personality and cultural perspectives on God's Word—which are all in Scripture, but some of which are more visible to certain people than to others—to bear on our prayers and how we formulate them.

Conclusion

There is much value in corporate prayer. But I think it's easier for people, when we get together for prayer, to do more talking than praying, and to focus our prayers in a "me-and-mine-centered" way rather than in a God-centered and Christ-centered way. What do you think would happen if all God's people cried out to him to bring about the fulfillment of his promises? If only we could learn how to pray together....

Follow-up

1. Do you pray together with fellow believers? Explain your answer with examples.
2. If you do, what if anything do you find difficult about it?
3. If you do, what if anything do you find unsatisfying about it?
4. If you do, what if anything do you find good or satisfying about it?
5. If you do, is there a sense of excitement in your group about praying together? Explain your answer.

6. If you pray together, how much time is spent in: talking, Bible Study, something else, and prayer? What do you think about these proportions?

7. If you don't pray together with other believers, what is keeping you from this? Consider prayerfully the power of synergy and look for opportunities to pray with God's people.

8. How much time does your church set aside for prayer in groups? How many people attend? What do you think about this?

Chapter 11

Pray with Your Spouse

I have the impression that Christian spouses rarely pray together regularly. I often ask men with whom I work if they regularly pray with their wives.[1] The answer I receive in most cases is that they do not or that they do so very little. Maybe this is because, in order to pray meaningfully with someone who knows you so well, you must maintain a relationship that reflects the love, honor and submission of the Trinity.[2]

This chapter focuses on prayer in marriage. I believe that Christian spouses should pray regularly together. Think of it as a meeting with the two of you before the Lord. If it is important for the body of Christ to pray together, how much more important is it for those who share the most intimate relationship God has created to do so.

Hindrances to Praying with Your Spouse

The Bible tells us of some typical hindrances to prayer with your spouse. The apostle Peter says,

In the same way, you wives, be submissive to your own husbands so that even if any of them are disobedient to the word, they may be won without a word by the behavior of their wives, as they observe your chaste and respectful behavior. Your adornment must not be merely external—braiding the hair, and wearing gold jewelry, or putting on dresses; but let it be the hidden person of the heart, with the imperishable quality of a gentle and quiet spirit, which is precious in the sight of God. For in this way in former times the holy women also, who hoped in God, used to adorn themselves, being submissive to their own husbands; just as Sarah obeyed Abraham, calling him lord, and you have become her children if you do what is right without being frightened by any fear. You husbands in the same way, live with your wives in an understanding way, as with someone weaker, since she is a woman; and show her honor as a fellow heir of the grace of life, so that your prayers will not be hindered.

   1 Peter 3:1-7 NASB 1995

William Hendriksen has the following comment on these verses:[3]

When a husband fails to live with his wife according to Scripture and does not respect her, he finds that he is unable to pray with her. Similarly, when a wife refuses to accept her husband's authority, she experiences an inability to pray with her spouse. God does not accept prayers that husband and wife offer in an atmosphere of strife and contention. He wants them to be reconciled so that they are able to pray together in peace and harmony and thus enjoy untold divine blessings.[4]

When a husband and wife do not treat each other according to God's design for marriage, they find it difficult to pray together. Wives should respect and submit to their husbands. A woman in my first church plant once told me, "I always submit to my husband, as long as he's right." She didn't mean "As long as he doesn't tell me to disobey the Lord." She meant, "As long as I agree with him." In Ephesians, Paul adds that wives should submit "in everything," and not just when you happen to agree with your husband.[5] This doesn't mean wives can't argue their case, and even do so forcefully. But when it comes to decision-making time, the Lord requires them to submit to their husbands as to the Lord.[6] How can you do this when you don't agree? By trusting the Lord to take care of you. In other words, you submit to the decision of your husband and trust that God is at work in this decision—as well as in all things—for your good.[7]

In addition, women must not find their sense of worth in external beauty or in what people think of them.[8] Of course, God made women to be beautiful, and in a fallen world, that's what men tend to focus on. Furthermore, in a fallen world women tend to respond to that kind of attention and so over focus on external beauty. But Peter says women are to focus on their character. They are to be gentle, like Jesus.[9] Gentleness is not the opposite of courage. Gentleness is not false-modesty, self-deprecation designed to get people to like you, or a spineless refusal to stand up for the truth. Being gentle doesn't mean a woman can't be industrious like the woman in Proverbs 31. No, gentleness is not the opposite of courage. In fact, it takes courage to be gentle in an evil world.[10] Rather, gentleness is the opposite of self-seeking. When the disciples argued among themselves about who was the greatest,[11] they were not being gentle. They weren't being gentle with each other, nor were they being gentle with the Samaritans, on whom they wanted to call down fire from heaven. In their self-seeking, they failed to discern that Jesus had come to bring justice through gentleness. As Isaiah had predicted:

Behold, My Servant, whom I uphold; My chosen one in whom My soul delights. I have put My Spirit upon Him; He will bring forth justice to the nations. He will not cry out or raise His voice, Nor make His voice heard in the street. A bruised reed He will not break and a dimly burning wick He will not extinguish; He will faithfully bring forth justice. He will not be disheartened or crushed Until He has established justice in the earth; And the coastlands will wait expectantly for His law.

Isaiah 42:1-4 NASB 1995

The prediction is that the Messiah would bring justice to this fallen world, and that he would do so gently: without calling attention to himself and without running roughshod over his people Israel who had failed in their mission and who were about to disappear as a nation. Of course, all believers are called to be gentle. But Peter emphasizes this character quality for wives. They should not resent their husband's authority. They should not compete with him for that authority. They should not allow fear of frightening things to push them into this self-seeking mode and thus keep them from doing what is right. They should not be self-seeking, but gentle.

Husbands should exercise their God-given authority in marriage in an understanding way. The King James Version translates this "according to knowledge," that is, according to Scripture.[12] This no doubt includes a Scriptural view of the way God made her. When a man does this, he will use his authority to exercise self-sacrificial responsibility. He will not use his authority to manipulate, control or use his wife to honor himself, but to honor, care for, praise[13] and protect his wife. He must use his leadership to provide an atmosphere in which the whole family can thrive in the Lord. He must love his wife as Jesus loves the church—being willing, if necessary, to sacrifice himself for her progress in becoming more like Christ. In doing this he shows that he believes his authority does not make him better, but that they are equal--heirs together of the grace of life.

Let me give an example in the area of decision-making. When after open discussion there is still disagreement, the husband must make a decision and take responsibility for it. Let's say they are planning a vacation. The husband wants to go to the mountains to go skiing, while the wife wants to go to the beach. The husband decides (objectively before the Lord, hopefully) that they should go to the beach. When they get there, it rains the whole time. If the husband says or implies by his actions, "See, I told you so. You should have listened to me," then he hasn't taken Biblical responsibility for his decision. Authority and responsibility go together.

On the other hand, let's say the husband decides (objectively before the Lord, hopefully) that they should go to the mountains. When they get there, they find that it didn't snow as expected. If the wife says or implies by her actions, "See, I told you so. You should have listened to me," then she has not properly submitted to his authority.

If husbands and wives are not fulfilling these God-given roles at least to the best of their ability at whatever level of spiritual maturity they find themselves, they will find it difficult to pray together in a meaningful and helpful way. In fact, there's a very good chance that if you find it difficult to pray with your spouse, you aren't fulfilling these roles.

Many people will respond to this by saying, "But my spouse isn't fulfilling his (her) role, and that makes it hard for me to fulfill mine." True, that does make it more difficult. But God isn't going to tell you that it's fine to hold off on fulfilling your role until your spouse gets his/her act together in this regard. In fact, fulfilling your role is the best way to help your spouse fulfill his/hers.

I find that most escalating tensions between spouses boil down to this: one or both of the spouses feels unloved or disrespected. The argument might apparently be over something else. But usually behind the surface argument is something of which they are not fully aware: one or both spouses feel the other is not fulfilling his/her God-given role in marriage.

The situation is exacerbated when one spouse tries to pressure the other into fulfilling his/her role—usually by withholding love/respect. What such a person is saying in effect through this pressure is this: "I won't fulfill my role until you fulfill yours." "I will love you when you respect me." "I will respect you when you demonstrate that you love me." In a serious escalating argument, very often both spouses are doing this to each other.

By acting this way, they show that their strength to love and respect depends, not on the Lord, but on their spouse. Acting this way is a rejection of Christ and the power of the Spirit to love and respect "in spite of" the way one's spouse is acting. Trusting Christ, and therefore not allowing one's ability to love depend on the love/respect of one's spouse, is one of the main ways married couples can apply faith in Christ to their marriage.

Under such unbiblical conditions, it probably feels easier to pray either by yourself or with someone who doesn't know you that well, and with whom you are not that close. However, the potential meaningfulness of prayer in those situations might be less. If you are unable to pray with your spouse, how meaningful can prayer alone or with others be?

Suggestions on How to Pray with Your Spouse

If I could give just one piece of advice to Christian married couples it would be this: make a habit of praying together in a meaningful way. Men, I urge you to take the leadership and to pray regularly with your wives. Make it a daily habit. Make it a priority. People usually have time for what is important to them. Here are some suggestions for men:

1. Make a commitment to start praying together. Even if there are tensions that might discourage you from praying together, committing to pray together--and beginning to do so--can be a good way to start dealing with them.
2. Get alone with your wife. Consider taking a walk together as you talk and pray.[14] Find a time and place in which you can minimize interruptions.

3. If there is tension between you, deal with it first. Ask for and give forgiveness as necessary. Don't let these tensions build up. Deal with them as they come up.

4. Don't create an atmosphere of a classroom with you as the teacher. Create a relaxed atmosphere of mutual learning before the Lord.

5. Ask your wife what is on her heart and mind. Talk about it. Make sure you understand her concerns, why they are concerns, and important implications of those concerns. This will help you pray more meaningfully.

6. Tell her what is on your heart and mind. Also strive for mutual understanding.

7. Bring Scripture to bear on your concerns. Create an atmosphere in which both feel free to do so.

8. Pray for these concerns.

9. Focus your prayers in a God-centered, Christ-centered, kingdom-centered way.

10. You might pray for each concern after it has been expressed and talked about. Or you might express all concerns and then pray for all of them afterward.

It is difficult to pray together if tensions in your marriage are not dealt with Biblically. But praying and reading the Bible together regularly in a way that is related to the specifics of your lives is one of the best things you can do for each other, for your children, and for those to whom you minister.

The Wonder of it All

Throughout this book I have attempted to show the wondrous role of prayer in the life of believers. Because of the closeness of husband and wife, praying together as a couple can be even more wondrous. Let me suggest four reasons:

1. It promotes a more deeply meaningful marriage. The key to your unity as a couple—the meaningfulness of your marriage—is found in your relationship with Christ and his plan for you as a team of kingdom agents. Talking together to the Father through Christ with the help of the Spirit as you face the opportunities and challenges before you is an important way to experience the fulness of the unity that God designed for marriage.

2. It promotes increased understanding and wisdom. As you study God's Word together and then decide on the implications for prayer, your understanding of God's Word is enriched and your wisdom about how to apply it increases.

3. It promotes decisions that advance God's kingdom. Praying together around God's Word enables you to keep your priorities straight as a couple and as a family. It provides the kingdom perspective you need to discern the things that take priority and make productive and wise decisions.

4. It provides insight into the meaning of life. The unity and diversity of the Trinity is both a mystery and a revelation to us of how God made us and the world. More than any other creation of God, marriage is designed to give us insight into this mystery. When two people get married, the two become one (Genesis 2:24)—a clear reflection of the unity and diversity of the Trinity. As a married couple prays together in a Biblical way about the situations they face, they gain greater insight into the mystery of the Trinity and how this unity and diversity should work in every sphere of life.

* * *

Follow-up

1. If you are married, do you pray regularly with your spouse? If not, make a commitment to do so.
2. If you do, how often and for how long each time? If you need to improve in this area, talk with your spouse and with God about doing that.
3. If you do pray with your spouse, how do you go about it? Is there anything you would like to change? Talk with your spouse about any changes you and he/she think might be helpful.
4. If you have experienced the wondrous nature of praying with your spouse, describe what it has been like and how it has been beneficial.
5. If you do not pray regularly with your spouse, why not?
6. Are you willing to make it a priority around which other things flow? I urge you to make it a priority.
7. If you are not married but want to be, look for someone who will value praying with you regularly.
8. If you are not married, you can still benefit from praying with a group of close friends. The closer you are to the people in this group, the more relational issues can either promote or detract from effective prayer.

Chapter 12

Pray with Expectancy

Where we used to live on Lookout Mountain, it's not uncommon for the fog to come rolling in and greatly reduce visibility. Sometimes you can't see more than a few feet in front of you. Something similar, I think, is happening to the church in the US. The fog of collective unbelief has been rolling in, reducing our ability to carry out the mission of the church in effective ways. The fog goes hand in hand with a lack of expectancy in prayer. Most Christians sincerely believe that when Christ comes there will be a multitude of believers from every tribe and nation standing before God's throne and praising him. But for all practical purposes, they don't believe that God will do anything truly significant for the advance of his kingdom where they live, in their neighborhood, at their place of employment, or even in their life and church. There is a lack of expectancy in prayer. The kingdom has come! It will come in its fullness. But when God's people don't really expect what God has promised, that's a form of unbelief; and unbelief calls for prayers of repentance and faith.

When Godly People Fail to Expect Much from God

Zechariah the priest was a godly man. Luke says of him and his wife, Elizabeth,

> They were both righteous in the sight of God, walking blamelessly in all the commandments and requirements of the Lord.
> Luke 1:6 NASB 1995

Elizabeth was barren in a time when barrenness was looked down upon. Some even thought of it as a sign of God's disfavor. Zechariah and Elizabeth had been praying for a child, but it seems they gradually lost hope as they grew older. In God's providence, Zechariah had been chosen by lot for a once-in-a-lifetime privilege: to enter the temple and burn incense.[1] During that process he would offer a prayer for the peace—that is salvation—of Israel as the people prayed outside. Suddenly, the angel Gabriel appeared to Zechariah and he was gripped with fear.[2] The angel said,

> "Do not be afraid, Zechariah, for your prayer has been heard, and your wife Elizabeth will bear you a son, and you shall name him John. 14 You will have joy and gladness, and many will rejoice over his birth. For he will be great in the sight of the Lord; and he will drink no wine or liquor, and he will be filled with the Holy Spirit while still in his mother's womb. And he will turn many of the sons of Israel back to the Lord their God. And it is he who will go as a forerunner before Him in the spirit and power of Elijah, to turn the hearts of fathers back to their children, and the disobedient to the attitude of the righteous, to make ready a people prepared for the Lord."
> Luke 1:13-17 NASB 1995

Zechariah's response was as follows:

How will I know this? For I am an old man, and my wife is advanced in her years.

Luke 1:18 NASB 1995

God was answering both of his prayers—for a child and for the peace of Israel. Because it was through the son of Zechariah and Elizabeth that God would prepare the way for the promised Messiah. We know his response was not motivated by a desire to have small faith strengthened as in the case of the man who said, "I do believe; help my unbelief!"[3] We know this because of the way the angel responded, rebuking him for his lack of faith.

The Bible makes it clear in this passage that it's possible to be a godly person in many ways, and yet to fail when it comes to expecting in faith for God to fulfill his promises to them, in their family, neighborhood, church, city, and country. Maybe they believe God will someday and, in some places, fulfill his promises, but not here and now.

Collective and Individual Unbelief

When Jesus spoke against whole cities, he was challenging collective unbelief. This has to do with the ways cultural[4] assumptions about what is true and important are embedded in the structures of society. So, for example, when a culture makes an idol out of freedom, and when this idea gets embedded into societal structures in the form of legal abortion clinics, you have a clear case of collective unbelief in God. Even though individuals within that society may not share the same idolatrous belief, or agree with the institutionalization of it, they are still influenced by it in many ways. In the first place, the practice becomes so commonplace, institutionalized and accepted among the general populace that it sometimes ceases to be as alarming as it should be. It's even difficult to recognize it for what it is. And even when dissenting individuals resist having their sensitivity dulled, the

153

effectiveness of their individual activities such as praying for revival, evangelizing, providing a counter cultural system that encourages mothers considering abortion to think about alternatives, protesting and trying to influence decision makers to change the law, are often dampened by the collective unbelief. The cultural system is so over-whelmingly strong and has such momentum that unless God inter-venes, change is not going to happen. The kind of change we want requires a revival sweeping through a whole nation.[5] I say all this to illustrate what I mean by collective unbelief.

Collective unbelief within our evangelical churches is not usually as strong as that of the society at large. But it is still there impeding our ability to be salt and light in a culture that is increasingly turning its back on God. Our ecclesiastical unbelief has to do with the design and implementation of our ministry systems in ways that show we don't really expect God to do much of anything in our day and place. Again, this is not the same as individual unbelief, although collective unbelief promotes individual unbelief. To remain faithful individu-ally in the midst of collective unbelief is like swimming upstream.[6] You find yourself isolated from the potential power of the group. The church was meant to function as a body. The synergy that the Spirit produces within the body as they collectively put their faith to work is a powerful spiritual force for the full coming of God's kingdom. Collective unbelief tends to make the church into a collection of indi-viduals who, while they might meet together for some purposes, for the most part work in an isolated manner. I still see faith in most Biblical churches. But I also see the fog of collective unbelief rolling in. Many churches find themselves in the position of the man who said to Jesus, "I believe. Help my unbelief."[7] But others simply don't expect God to do much at all.

What God Has Done and Promised

Before I talk more specifically about the collective unbelief I see in many churches, I want to remind us of some of the things God has done and has promised to do in Christ and through the Spirit.

1. In Christ the kingdom has come, though not yet in its fullness. God through Christ has dealt once and for all with death, the evil one, and the sin of his people.[8] He has cast our sins into the depths of the sea. No scuba diving allowed.

2. God through Christ has brought us into a relationship with himself such that the Father is smiling on us, and we have free access into his presence.[9] So many people view the Heavenly Father as angry and distant. But he sings over us with joy.[10]

3. He has given us 66 books from his own hand to tell us the truth and keep us on the right track.

4. Jesus is now the human king of the world—the promised heir of David's throne. He has poured out the Holy Spirit in and among his people to equip us with the greatest power in the universe to do what would otherwise be impossible: bring in the fullness of his kingdom.[11] We are his kingdom agents through whom he brings his plan to completion. We are God's elite Impossible Mission Force, empowered by his Spirit, and engaged in the greatest adventure of all time. As we drink of Christ— that is, put our faith to work—the Holy Spirit flows out from us like a powerful river to accomplish God's otherwise impossible mission.[12] One sip of Jesus and rivers flow out. That's how God accomplishes the impossible through his people. When we look away from ourselves to Christ and thus put our faith to work, he unleashes the power of his Spirit to bring his kingdom.

5. Christ has given his people gifts, not so we can feel good about ourselves, but so we can be useful in his plan to bring in the fullness of his kingdom.[13]

6. God is training his people through the challenges we face to be increasingly useful in this process of bringing in the fullness of his kingdom. When we are going through difficult circumstances, we often wonder why he seems so distant. Very often it's the case that he is like a coach preparing us for battle. And that is never easy and rarely pleasant.[14] But just as athletes are willing to train their bodies to gain the prize, so we should be willing to be trained for advancing God's kingdom.

7. Jesus sat down at the right hand of the Father to pray for us his people. He is the Pray-er-in-Chief. He prays for us, not primarily for our comfort (although he is also concerned[15] about that), but so our faith will grow and not fail; so we will have increasing power to bring about his otherwise impossible plan.[16] Do you think the Father will listen to the intercession of Jesus on our behalf? Of course he will!

8. The Holy Spirit helps us in our weakness by interpreting our less than perfect prayers before the throne of grace in a way that perfectly fits with God's will.[17]

9. Jesus, having sat down at the right hand of the Father, has us *anchored* to himself. Even if the mountains fall into the depths of the sea, he will continue to do all these things for us and finally bring us to himself. Nothing can harm us because he turns everything--even death--around for our good. We of all people should be carefree and fearless. We should be characterized by bold humility.[18]

10. When Christ comes back again, there will be a multitude so numerous standing before the throne of God and praising him that no one will be able to count it. The multitude will include people from every tribe, nation,

and language.[19] We know the outcome of this greatest adventure of all time. Jesus has won and will work out all the implications of his victory—largely through his people.

These are wonderful actions and promises! To the extent that we take them seriously we should be in awe of what he has done and promises to do.

Signs of Collective Unbelief

I'll mention a few examples of how I see ministry systems reflecting assumptions and structures that reveal some degree (not usually total) of collective unbelief. Remember also that collective unbelief doesn't necessarily tell you about the spiritual condition of the individual, who may be very godly. But even godly people who are operating in the fog of collective unbelief are hindered. The rivers of life that are supposed to be flowing out are clogged up to some extent.

1. *Preaching*: Much preaching I've heard does not intentionally strive to put people in awe of Christ and thus has little power to evoke faith that results in audacious prayers and bold humility. Just telling people to trust Christ and not themselves cannot evoke faith in the way presenting the glory of Christ will. Furthermore, we often hear the totally proper reminder that we are justified by faith so don't trust in your works for salvation, and the equally legitimate call to continually rest in our once-for-all justification by faith. But we rarely hear the exhortation to put our faith to work on the basis of what God has done and is doing in Christ and by the Spirit. As a result, people tend to reinterpret the intended message within a culture-centric frame that says, "OK, I'll trust in Christ and not myself. Just don't tell me I have to be bold

and go out there and do stuff." Why, if we are preaching Christ, is there not more excitement about him and about engaging in the greatest adventure of all time?

2. *Teaching*: In my circles, which emphasize correct doctrine (and in my opinion our doctrine is excellent), spiritual growth is assumed to be the result of intellectually assimilating information that comes from the leaders as they explain the Bible. It is assumed that merely understanding concepts leads to proper action and to growth in character. While there is some truth to this, the assumption minimizes corollary truths: for example, that you can't really understand until by God's grace you put something into practice.[20] And that your understanding grows as your love grows.[21] The covenantal connection in Christ among concept, action and character (love) is for the most part ignored. The assumption that growth is basically a one-way street—concepts leading to action and character--is practically an idolatry of knowledge. People assume that, since I've heard the truth and accept it as truth, whatever I'm doing must be what that knowledge produces. As a result, people can remain passive, but confident that everything is OK because they "know" the truth. When you think of what God has promised and compare it with what we see, it leads to this question: why is the focus on correct doctrine producing so little fruit?

3. *Meeting People*: Many Christians don't have non-Christian friends or acquaintances with whom they have a significant relationship. Unlike Jesus, who often hung out with sinners, we often have no opportunities to share the gospel because we have no significant contact with them. Jesus gave us the Spirit to reach out to others. Why is that not happening?

4. *Evangelism*: Why are there so few adult baptisms in so many churches that teach the truth of God's Word? Church growth happens more by people moving from one city to another and joining a new church, or by one church attracting people from another church by creating more interesting programs. If God has so many people out there that no one can count them, surely there are people in our neighborhoods, towns and cities who have not yet heard. If we refuse to get up off our seats and find them, the Lord may just pass us by and use someone else to accomplish his kingdom purposes.

5. *Prayer*: In my circles, prayer meetings are not very well attended. Most prayer meetings are infused with a circumstantial perspective, and even a me-and-mine mentality. We present a list of things we want God to do for us. As a result, prayer meetings are usually somewhat boring. While it's not wrong to ask God for things we need ("give us this day our daily bread") where is the insisting that God fulfill all his promises regarding the full coming of his kingdom. Didn't he tell us to pray: "Your kingdom come"? Jesus said, "Ask anything in my name and I will do it." Do we really believe it? The practice of reminding God of his promises, his character, of what he has done for his people, and then placing the requests within that context is all but forgotten. The practice of giving God Biblical reasons for what we request has greatly diminished. The ability to pray specifically within this kingdom perspective is rare. In addition, many prayer meetings are really Bible studies, with some time dedicated to talking about prayer requests, and a few minutes of prayer tacked on at the end. I suspect this is because we really don't know how to pray.

6. *Fellowship*: Fellowship has been reduced to eating together and chatting about whatever comes to mind. I'm not against chit-chat, but when fellowship gets reduced to chit-chat, something has gone wrong. The fellowship of God's people is a powerful weapon that God uses to bring in the fullness of his kingdom. The synergy that results from people getting to know each other, enjoying each other, learning from one another, and serving each other, ends up having a tremendous impact on those around us. Churches should think about the intersections of fellowship and mission, of fellowship and evangelism, of fellowship and teaching/learning, of fellowship and service, of fellowship and worship, of fellowship and prayer.

7. *Service*: Where are the churches that back up their words with actions in the community? This probably happens more than evangelism, but it often takes place in a way that is divorced from communicating God's Word and from significant relationship. For example, you could give money for the needy without ever getting involved with people in service. I believe that the lack of integration of word and deed takes away from our credibility within the church's context.

8. *Leadership*: Many churches go one of two ways: (1) pressuring people to get involved in programs to such an extent that they get burned out, or (2) telling people, "If you have a problem let me know. Otherwise, I'll leave you alone." Ephesians 4 says the job of leaders is to "equip" the saints so they can do ministry. In the Greek, this word means "to make complete." It involves more than just teaching classes or otherwise passing along information. Leadership means explicitly pointing people to Christ, to his great promises, to the great adventure and mission to which he has called us. It involves modeling ministry,

watching people do ministry and giving them feedback, and getting involved with people. It includes investing in people—making disciples—rather than either pressuring them or leaving them alone. Why are there so few elders who really believe--and put into practice--Ephesians 4?

9. *Mission*: The mission of the church is reduced to cross-cultural "missions." Churches in our culture are often more engaged in maintenance and growth through transfer than in the mission of the church. Many "missions[22]" conferences are set up (unintentionally) in a way that provokes astonishment at exotic and poor conditions, rather than focusing on the astonishment that the person and work of Christ can evoke in us, or on what the sending churches can learn from churches in other cultures. The focus of the "missions" conference is on the missionary giving a stirring report of his/her activities[23] As a result, people are often moved to give and go more though a sense of guilt at having so much in comparison with many others in the world than by being in awe of Christ and wanting to get involved in his kingdom adventure.

10. *Worldview Living*: In my experience, Christians typically understand the word "worldview" to refer to one's Christian system of *thought*. We should distinguish, however, between an *espoused* Christian worldview and a Christian worldview *in-use*. The latter is identified more by our *actions* than by our beliefs alone. More specifically, it is best identified through the observed integration in Christ of our beliefs, actions and character. I would like to point out one particular area in which I see weakness in the prevailing Christian worldview-in-use. Most preachers do not apply God's Word to all areas of life. If indeed they do make practical applications in their sermons, these applications are typically confined to

individual or interpersonal attitudes and actions—most often within the church. Very rarely do you hear preachers applying Scripture to the signs of unbelief in this list, or to cultural or political issues.[24] While it's true that the church should not identify itself with any political party—because our identity is in Christ, and we are agents of his kingdom—church leaders should be giving their congregations Biblical guidance on the cultural and political issues we face every day. The great blessings our nation has experienced in the past were the result of the influence of the gospel and a Christian worldview. The beneficial effects of that worldview are currently being dismantled by demonic forces operating through people they influence and even control. One gets the impression that church leaders refrain from addressing these issues clearly for fear of losing members or for fear of being labeled a hater. In the Biblical worldview, truth and love come together in Christ. Many in the church have fallen into a kind of idolatry of love that suppresses the truth out of fear. Our culture—by misconstruing the original intent of the separation of church and state—has told the church to stay in its "spiritual" lane and not interfere with things outside the church. Unfortunately, the church has by and large [25]obeyed. One result is that the church has limited its ability to be the salt of the earth and the light of the world. No other organization can fulfill this function. It has been given to the church. But if the church refuses to fulfill that mission out of fear, then the whole world will suffer.

A Call to Pray for Renewal of Expectancy

I believe the assumptions behind these distorted ministry designs reflect a collective unbelief. There may be very godly people working in the church. That's not the issue I'm bringing to the fore. Godly people may be working within systems that reflect collective unbelief. Even godly people need to examine their ministry systems and consider the extent to which these reflect collective unbelief. Some churches may find collective unbelief in only some of these systems. Other churches may find that all these systems reflect collective unbelief. They often go together and reinforce each other. If you find that your church ministry systems reflect no collective unbelief, then rejoice and pray for the many churches that are affected by it. Pray for a renewal of the church in our day.

There is hope for churches that find themselves caught in the restricting web of collective unbelief: God's promises are still true. The prayer of repentance for collective unbelief and renewed faith in God's promises will enable churches to examine their ministry designs and redesign them with more Biblical assumptions that move them out to engage in God's mission. God has done great things in Christ. On the basis of what he has done in Christ, he has promised great things during the Now-But-Not-Yet and beyond. We should expect nothing less. May we pray with expectancy! According to Psalm 2, God has placed his king on the eschatological version of Mount Zion[26]. The kingdom has come—even though not yet in its fullness. Jesus is even now the human king of the world. Expect God to do what he says he will do through him!

Follow-up

1. Do you find it difficult to expect that God will really do much in your place and your time? Explain your answer with examples. If necessary, repent of your unbelief.

2. What do you expect God to do in your life? In your church? In your city?

3. Have you been praying for these things? Has your church been praying for them?

4. What has been your experience of having a divine person —the Holy Spirit—live inside you and be with you wherever you are and whatever you do? What difference has the presence of the Holy Spirit made in your life?

5. Do you see a need for an awakening in your church? In your denomination? Either way, explain why.

Appendix A: Prayer Meetings

What would a healthy prayer meeting look like? Really, it could take many different forms. I'll offer a few ideas, but I don't mean to imply that this is the only way to go about having a prayer meeting.

In the first place it helps if the people praying together are involved in some ministry together (See Chapter 9). The lack of this experiential knowledge is a significant obstacle to meaningful prayer meetings. Obviously, I don't mean that everyone has to be involved in everything. But the more people are involved in action together, the more meaningful their prayer together will be. At a bare minimum, if the people at least know with some specificity what is happening in the various ministries of the church, and if they are involved in at least some way, that will help.

Generally, prayer should include adoration of God, confession of sin, giving thanks to God, and requests. These can all be found in the Lord's prayer[1]. These are often separated, but I don't think that's necessary. In some ways it seems unnatural to separate them completely into four different prayer times. We don't talk to each other that way. In everyday talk, expressions of appreciation, thanks, requests and confession are typically intermingled.

I suggest the following to help focus prayer requests. Depending on the group, some of these questions may be too invasive to ask of others, but you could ask them of yourself, and you can ask informational questions of others that may get at the following:

1. *The What*: When you bring up a prayer request, ask yourself, "What are we really praying for here? Who are the people involved? What is the main issue? What are other related issues? Have people ask questions so you can look at it from various perspectives until you feel you really understand what the issue is, or what the issues are. It may seem obvious at first, but if you think about it together you may be surprised how the prayer request comes into better focus.

2. *The Why*: Ask yourself, "Why do we want to ask this of the Lord? What does it have to do with his kingdom—its presence now and its full coming?" What would be the consequences if it weren't answered? Have people ask questions and offer various perspectives on why it is important to make this request. The "why" might seem obvious at first, but if you discuss it together, you may be surprised at how it comes into better focus.

3. *The Reasons*: Ask yourself, "What Biblical reasons can we offer to God as to why he should answer this request?" Again, have people offer different perspectives on this. Because of something God has done in the past? Because of something God has promised? Because of who his people are? Because of some command? Because of some attribute of God? Because of his providential leading? Because of something the enemy is doing? Because of someone's sin? Because of its effect on other things? I find that most people aren't used to giving Biblical reasons for their requests. So, this may be difficult at first. By doing this, you are having a kind of

Bible study. You are bringing the Bible study and the prayer requests together.

4. *The Related Kinds of Prayer*: Ask yourself, "Is there anything related to this request that we should be thankful for? Is there anything we should praise God for? Is there anything that needs to be confessed and repented of? Of course, adoration, confession and thanksgiving don't have to be connected to a request. But it's a good idea to see how requests might be related.

5. *The Attitudes*: Pray as an adventurer, as a warrior, with audacity, boldness, humility, earnestness and expectancy.

As you go through this process, you may find some differences of perspective arising among the various participants. If you don't understand the perspective someone offers, it's easy just to dismiss it. Rather, ask about it. "What do you mean by that?" This is one of the values of praying together. We learn from each other as we pray. We learn who God is, who we are, what is happening in our world, and how to pray about it.

As you're learning how to pray this way, it's often helpful to take one request at time. State the request, discuss it in the ways suggested above, and then pray together for that one request. Then go on to the next request. You may find you need more time to pray.

The process I suggest above can be done without talking about it beforehand, but it usually takes some experience. You might prefer to talk about your requests through the process of prayer.

Appendix B: Growing Your Faith

We have examined various aspects of prayer as it relates to our mission, all of which involve our faith. Since faith in Christ is so central to prayer and mission, this appendix will focus on the need for our faith to be always growing.

Believing from the Heart

What does it mean to *have faith*? Jesus said to his disciples,

> "Have faith in God. Truly, I say to you, whoever says to this mountain, 'Be taken up and thrown into the sea,' and does not doubt *in his heart*, but believes that what he says will come to pass, it will be done for him. Therefore I tell you, whatever you ask in prayer, believe that you have received it, and it will be yours.
> Mark 11:22-24 ESV

One of the things this verse teaches is that faith involves believing *from the heart*—just as doubting happens *"in the heart."* Although faith involves the intellect, it is not a *mere* intellectual belief. In the Bible the heart is the center of the mind, the will and the emotions. Having faith involves all three.

In 1521, Philip Melanchthon (one of the Reformers), published a book entitled *Loci communes theologici,* in which he defined three aspects of saving faith using these Latin words: *notitia, assensus,* and *fiducia. Notitia* has to do with intellectually believing correct doctrine. *Assensus* has to do with the engagement of the will in the sense of a commitment to act on the truth. *Fiducia* involves personal trust. These three together, then, help us understand what it means to belief from the heart: with mind, will and emotions. Figure 1 illustrates this truth.

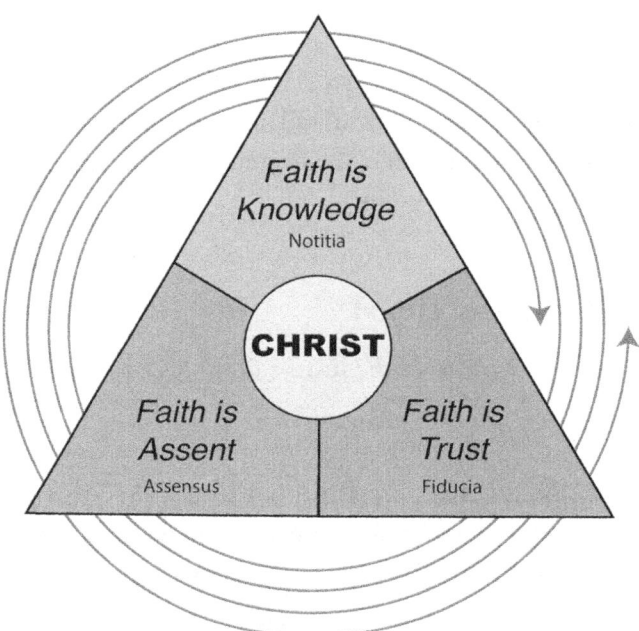

Figure 10. The Three Aspects of Faith

A Gift from God

Believing from the heart is not something we can conjure up or produce ourselves in any way. It must come from God. When a person is regenerated, God gives that person the gift of faith. Paul says,

> For by grace you have been saved through faith; and this is not your own doing, it is the gift of God; not a result of works, so that no one may boast.
> Ephesians 2:8-9 ESV

This gift of faith includes all three aspects: *notitia, assensus* and *fiducia*.

Focus on the Object of Faith

The "amounts" of each aspect we receive may be very small in the beginning. But Jesus has clarified to us that it's the *object* of our faith-- Jesus-- that is of primary importance, and not--in the first place--the amount or degree of faith. So, when the disciples asked Jesus to increase their faith, he gave them a surprising answer:

> The apostles said to the Lord, "Increase our faith!" And the Lord said, "If you had faith like a grain of mustard seed, you could say to this mulberry tree, 'Be uprooted and planted in the sea,' and it would obey you.
> Luke 17:5-6 ESV

The point is that a mustard seed is very small. Jesus can and will do great things through even a small faith.

The Necessity of Faith

On the other hand, when there is a lack of faith Jesus often "can't" and/or "won't" do anything. For example, in Nazareth Jesus "did not do many miracles...due to their lack of faith."[1] Of the same situation Mark says,

> "He could not do any miracles there.... He was amazed at their lack of faith.
>> Mark 6:5-6 ESV

Of course, God is sovereign and can do what he wants, but somehow where there is a certain kind of unbelief he apparently does not and somehow "cannot" do the work that he does when faith is present to any degree.

The Importance of a Growing Faith

On the other hand, the Lord expects our faith to grow and become more effective. Jesus sometimes told his disciples that they had "little faith," the implication being that they should have greater faith. Here are two examples:

> .... there arose a great storm on the sea, so that the boat was being swamped by the waves; but he was asleep. And they went and woke him, saying, "Save us, Lord; we are perishing." And he said to them, "Why are you afraid, O you of little faith?" Then he rose and rebuked the winds and the sea, and there was a great calm.
>> Matthew 8:24-26 ESV
>
> So Peter got out of the boat and walked on the water and came to Jesus. But when he saw the wind, he was afraid, and beginning to sink he cried out, "Lord, save me." Jesus immedi-

ately reached out his hand and took hold of him, saying to him, "O you of little faith, why did you doubt?"
Matthew 14:29-31 ESV

Humanly speaking, both of these events are drastic, life-and-death situations. Yet Jesus' attitude is, "It's obvious you should not be afraid or doubt. I'm here! You have no excuse!" And since he is now with us in a closer and better way[2] through the indwelling Spirit, we should also not doubt or have merely "little faith."

Cultivating Faith

So, we should not be content with the initial gift of faith. Once we receive this gift, it is our responsibility to *cultivate* it so we become more effective kingdom agents and are able to enjoy God more.

So how do you cultivate faith? You cultivate it by using one aspect of faith to enhance another. So, in the first place you cultivate faith by studying Scripture to increase and clarify your conceptual understanding of the truth and to identify and reject false (often hidden and culturally acquired) beliefs. You also cultivate faith by putting your faith to work in new, different and often more challenging situations. In the third place, you also cultivate your faith by experiencing and developing a relationship with Christ and so trusting him more.

These three aspects of faith are designed to enhance each other. Having correct intellectual belief enhances putting it to work and trusting Christ. Trusting Christ clarifies and confirms the value of intellectual belief and encourages us to put our faith to work. Putting our faith to work gives us experience in using faith, thus clarifying and confirming our intellectual belief and encouraging us to trust Christ more. The following interactions show how faith can be cultivated:

1. The more you understand (*notitia*), the more you will be able to obey (*assensus*) and trust (*fiducia*).
2. The more you obey (*assensus*), the more you will be able to understand (*notitia*) and trust (*fiducia*).
3. The more you trust (*fiducia*), the more you will be able to understand (*notitia*) and obey (*fiducia*).

Some Christians are so overly focused on understanding the truth of the Bible that they need to get out and put their faith to work in specific ways, and/or spend more time in prayer and fellowship with others. Make a plan to pray for more than 5 minutes a day. Set aside some significant time to be alone with the Lord. Or reach out to a neighbor. Invite someone who isn't a close friend to your home for a meal. Do something like this as a way of putting your faith to work in practical ways.

Other Christians are so overly focused on doing things for the Lord that they have neglected to study God's Word and spend time talking with him in prayer. Make a plan to study the Bible seriously—whether on your own or with others. Think about its implications for your life. Spend an hour in prayer—or start with a half hour if an hour seems overwhelming.

Still other Christians are so overly focused on developing their relationship with the Lord—through prayer, through reading devotional books, or through participation in small groups that focus on this that they have neglected to read God's Word more in depth or put their faith to work in practical ways.

In short, one of the main ways to cultivate your faith is to intentionally put each aspect of faith to work to enhance and grow the others. Start by focusing on the neglected aspects. The relationship among the three should be synergistic such that each enhances the other. But if you are neglecting one or more of these aspects of faith, you will miss out on this synergistic growth of faith.

Growing Your Weak Faith

What should you do if you find yourself, either in a state of practical unbelief or in a state of little faith? I suggest the following:[3]

1. Repent of your lack of faith and ask the Lord to help you cultivate your faith.
2. Repent, if necessary, for having lived by points--for having been captivated by your culture and its values.
3. Discovering the extent to which you have been captivated by the culture will probably be a process that will take time because cultural captivity often happens below the level of awareness. Interact with Christians from different cultures or sub-cultures in order to learn from their experience with the Lord.
4. Pray, asking the Lord to help you become more aware of the ways you may have been captivated by your culture and to help you in the process of growth so you can make better progress.
5. Remind yourself of who Christ is and what he has done. It's a vision of the glory of Christ that evokes faith in us.
6. Cultivate your faith as described above by putting the three aspects of faith to work as a means of enhancing the others.
7. Find a group of people who are like-minded and who will support each other in this process.

Having faith is not a matter of convincing yourself to believe something. It's not merely a matter of knowing your Bible really well. It's not taking on the behaviors of someone who has great faith. Even the growth of faith is a gift of God. But he normally makes it grow through our diligent cultivation of it. Faith grows through the process of daily and consistent cultivation with the support of God's people.

Be honest as you evaluate your level of faith and give yourself to its cultivation with the support of God's people.

Appendix C: The Use of Logic in Interpretation

Most theologians affirm that we sometimes encounter mystery when it comes to our knowledge of God and his ways. For example, there are doctrines that on the surface might seem to contradict each other. How is it that God can be both one and three? In this sense the doctrine of the Trinity is mysterious. Maybe the doctrine of the trinity is the kind of mystery we see in Pauline literature: something that was not revealed in the past but that can be revealed later. Maybe when we are glorified God will reveal to us in what sense he is one and in what sense he is three and it will all make better sense. On the other hand, maybe there are mysteries that we will never penetrate just because we are not God. As Isaiah says,

> For my thoughts are not your thoughts,
>> neither are your ways my ways, declares the Lord.
> For as the heavens are higher than the earth,
>> so are my ways higher than your ways
>> and my thoughts than your thoughts.
> *Isaiah 55:8-9 NASB 1995*

When it comes to mysteries in the Bible in which two doctrines might seem to contradict each other but are both presented as true, it's very often the case that some people give full weight to one of the teachings and as a result don't give full weight to the other. They define the second in light of the first instead of allowing the Biblical text to define each. I'd like to focus on these two doctrines whose relationship is somewhat mysterious.

1. God in his sovereignty has an eternal plan made before creation and according to which he foreordains whatever comes to pass. Creation, the fall, redemption and consummation are all included in this plan.
2. God holds people accountable for their actions, punishing the wicked and rewarding those who are faithful to him.

Theological Error #1

People fall into theological error--I'll call this Theological Error #1-- when they rightly give full weight to the Biblical teaching on God's sovereignty, but then make logical deductions from that teaching— deductions that limit the full impact of the Biblical data on man's responsibility.

For example, some people say that since the fall was part of God's eternal plan, Adam really had no choice but to sin. Things could not have been otherwise because the fall was part of God's eternal plan which always comes to pass. For these people, the locus of mystery is this:

1. God foreordains whatever comes to pass including the fall. This means that the fall had to happen because it was part of God's plan.
2. Even though things could not have been otherwise, Adam is still somehow responsible for his sin.

I would call this a contradiction. It says that Adam had no choice but to sin, yet he is held responsible for his decision. I believe these people have misplaced the locus of mystery. I would formulate the mystery this way:

God foreordains whatever comes to pass including the fall.

Adam had a real choice and things could have been otherwise, but he chose to sin and is therefore responsible.

I believe this formulation takes the Biblical data more seriously. For example, the Bible makes it clear in various places that things could have been different if people had obeyed. After David sinned by killing Uriah and taking Bathsheba to be his wife, God said,

> I also gave you your master's house and *put* your master's wives into your care, and I gave you the house of Israel and Judah; and if *that had been* too little, I would have added to you many more things like these!
> *2 Samuel 12:8 NASB 1995*

In other words, if David had refrained from sinning, God would have blessed him even more than he had up to that point. Here's another example. God says to his covenant people:

> If only you had paid attention to My commandments! Then your well-being would have been like a river, And your righteousness like the waves of the sea.
> *Isaiah 48:18 NASB 1995*

In other words, things could have been otherwise if they had obeyed. Those who fall into Theological Error #1 have to somehow explain away the full impact of these verses. Often, they say that when God says things like this, you can't take him literally. He is merely condescending to our human frailty and explaining things in a way that makes sense to us. But that explanation makes no sense. Is

God--who made man in his image--not capable of communicating with us clearly?

I'll give one more example. On the one hand, the Father is said to know the day and time of Jesus' coming (Matthew 24:36).[1] On the other hand, Peter says believers in his audience can speed up his coming (2 Peter 3:10-12). If we try to explain away the full force of the second part of the verse by saying something like "It just seems to us like it's speeding up," we fall into Theological Error #1.

Theological Error #2

A similar error is made by those who give priority to man's responsibility and then dilute the full force of the teaching on God's sovereignty. Open Theists fall into this error when they limit God's knowledge and control in order to make room for the real significance of man's choices. Arminians also fall somewhat into this error when they insist that people are fully able to choose God on their own. God doesn't first have to change their hearts in order for them to believe. In both cases God's sovereignty is minimized in order to make room for the real significance of man's actions.[2]

Conclusion

The Bible calls us to use our God-given logic to order and understand Scripture. But it also calls us to submit our logic to Scripture when necessary. If the Bible affirms two things that seem not to go together, we may not be able to understand fully how they go together, but they are not therefore unintelligible. We can respond in faith and obedience to both instead of minimizing or explaining away one of them. In the context of this book, I want to emphasize the fact that the truth of God's sovereignty should not be used to eliminate or suppress the significance of our prayers. Our prayers can change things.

Appendix D: Why Christians Suffer

If the Bible teaches that obedience leads to blessing, why do Christians suffer? In the face of so much suffering, how do we make sense of verses like these?

> If you walk in My statutes and keep My commandments so as to carry them out, then I shall give you rains in their season, so that the land will yield its produce and the trees of the field will bear their fruit. Indeed, your threshing will last for you until grape gathering, and grape gathering will last until sowing time. You will thus eat your food to the full and live securely in your land. I shall also grant peace in the land, so that you may lie down with no one making you tremble. I shall also eliminate harmful beasts from the land, and no sword will pass through your land. But you will chase your enemies and they will fall before you by the sword; five of you will chase a hundred, and a hundred of you will chase ten thousand, and your enemies will fall before you by the sword. So I will turn toward you and make you fruitful and multiply you, and I will confirm My covenant with you. You

will eat the old supply and clear out the old because of the new.

Leviticus 26:3-10 NASB 1995

While these verses are certainly true, they convey one aspect of the truth. There are other factors at play as well. The following is designed to provide an idea of some of the other factors involved. Here are some of the main possibilities of why a Christian might be suffering.

1. As a judgment for some specific sin.[1] But if this is the case the Lord will let the person know. If we sincerely examine our hearts, he will not hide the reason of the judgment. In some cases, people have so damaged their conscience,[2] that they don't hear the Lord telling them. In that case they need help from fellow believers.
2. To help us grow by removing some sinful habit.[3] This is not judgment but discipline. It's proof that we are loved children of the Father. It should not lead to depression but to faith. In the moment it is not pleasant, but it produces good fruit.
3. To increase our hope in the glory of God.[4]
4. To increase our steadfastness.[5]
5. To increase our wisdom.[6]
6. To train us for greater effectiveness in God's kingdom.[7]
7. So we can comfort others who are suffering.[8]
8. To demonstrate our faith and faithfulness. Job suffered, not because he had sinned, but because he had been faithful. We don't know whether or not our faith works unless it is tested. After it's put to the test, it's even more useful, because we have experience using it.[9]
9. Believers bear the reproach of Christ. We participate in his sufferings because we are united to him in his death

and resurrection. Satan hates us because he hates Christ–
and we are united to him.[10]

10. Because we are God's kingdom agents involved in the
    greatest adventure of all time. Adventurers always face
    challenges that are usually painful.[11]

I believe that if we are suffering for reason 1, the Lord will not
hide it from us. He will work through our conscience and possibly the
testimony of others to let us know. If we are suffering for reason 2, he
will also let us know as we are ready to understand it.

Job's friends said he was suffering for reasons 1 and maybe 2. The
Bible says or implies he was suffering for other reasons.

Appendix E: The Rebound Movement and the Way of the Cross

The Basic Idea of the Rebound Movement

Soteriology begins in Genesis 3 with the "proto gospel." Here we see the pattern for the rest of Scripture in three elements: God takes the initiative toward his goal, Satan "bites" and everything looks black and hopeless, and then God intervenes with judgment and salvation in such a way that his plan is actually furthered. See Figure 11 below.

This is the "rebound" movement because the apparent downward movement experienced because of Satan's attack is overcome by a seemingly disproportionate upward and forward movement[1] of the kingdom through God's intervention.[2] He works all things together for the good of those who love him because he is at work in everything—even Satan's attacks—to bring about his purposes. Scripture is structured by this kind of rebound movement, which finds its climax in the cross of Christ.[3] The bite of the serpent turns out to be a furthering of God's plan as Jesus suffers in the place of his people.

Now the pattern continues as we his people walk the way of the cross. Paul says we have the privilege of suffering for Christ, and that he fills up his body the sufferings that are lacking. In other words,

God uses our suffering for the sake of the kingdom to further his purposes. Sometimes this suffering includes God showing us increasingly the ways in which sin lurks in our "flesh."

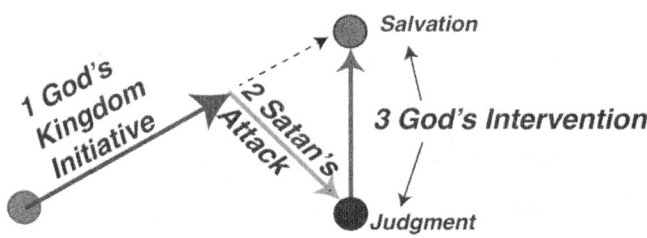

Figure 11. The Rebound Movement

The Primary Implications

Ministry is a lot messier than many people think it should be. Reformation often happens in the midst of suffering. We need to allow for this kind of "failure" and encourage each other in the midst of it. Although we should pray and plan for results, we should not judge our ministries only on the basis of visible results.

Furthermore, although the Lord obviously uses our gifts to further his kingdom work, there is an important sense in which he uses our weakness and death to accomplish his purposes. Missionaries (and all believers are to be missionaries) are those who are willing to allow the Lord to accomplish his purposes through their weaknesses and death. It is when we are weak that Christ's power rests upon us.

This principle applies not only to individuals, but also to organizations. Even mission organizations should be willing to walk the way of the cross. That is, they should be less concerned about their own survival as an organization and be willing to serve unto death. For evolutionary theories, survival is a core value. In God's kingdom, however, those who make survival a core value will not survive. The one who holds on to his life will lose it.

Sometimes we wonder what this or that problem or difficulty has to do with the kingdom and our ministry. We say, "Why is the Lord allowing this to happen? I came here to serve the Lord. What does this have to do with the kingdom?" From the point of view of the rebound movement, it has everything to do with it. We walk the way of the cross, the only path to the promised glory.

The Way of the Cross in the Sweep of Biblical History

Figure 12 below portrays the sweep of Biblical history from the point of view of the way of the cross. It includes some prominent examples of the rebound movement. The failures and judgments of God's people in the Old Testament (lines declining to the right) prefigure the final judgment that descends upon the Son of Man on the cross. After his death and resurrection, God's people are united to Christ and have the privilege of walking the way of the cross as they head for the glory of the fullness of the kingdom—the World to Come.

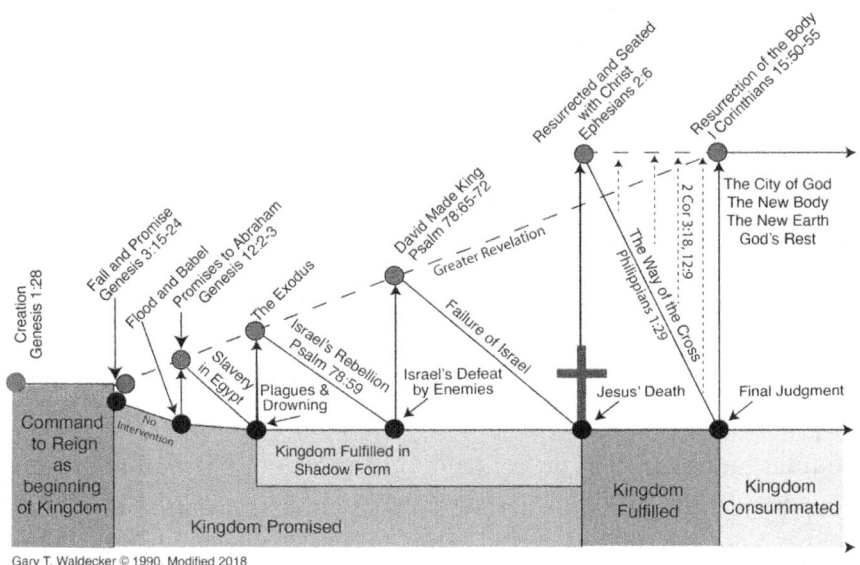

Gary T. Waldecker © 1990. Modified 2018

Figure 12. The Way of the Cross in the Sweep of Biblical History

Attacks Against the Offspring of the Godly Overruled

Because of the fall, God brings his kingdom by way of the cross. In Genesis 3:15, God promises that a descendent of Adam and Eve will crush the head of serpent, the evil one, under his feet. In this way he restores the kingdom rule of man. But the descendent will, in the process, be bitten on the heel by the serpent. Thus begins the way of the cross.

From that moment on, Satan attacks the offspring of the godly line. This attack is real, and it hurts. But in God's providence and plan of redemption, the attack always turns out to further the cause of his kingdom.

When Satan strikes by inciting Cain to kill his godly brother, God sends Cain out to wander. In his search for security and a name,

Cain builds a city. Although they do it for the wrong reasons, Cain and his descendants begin to develop the potential in God's creation.

The serpent strikes again when he gathers the descendants of Noah together to form a monolithic block of evil. In this way no godly children would be born. But God confuses their language and spreads them out to do cultural activity all over the world.

From the resulting nations, God calls Abraham and promises that kings will be among his descendants. Through Abraham God will bless all the nations of the world and so bring his kingdom.

When Joseph, one of Abraham's descendants, has dreams about ruling over the rest of his family, it looks like he is going to be the one to bring in the kingdom. Satan strikes and Joseph is sold as a slave by his jealous brothers. But this turns out to be a further blow to the evil one. God raises Joseph to power in Egypt so that he can save the godly line when a famine strikes the land. Judah, through whom the predicted descendent would come, is saved. In Egypt God's people become a large nation.

The Israelites were becoming so large, in fact, that the Pharaoh made a decree that all males born to the Israelites must die. But because of this decree the baby Moses, who would later be used of God to deliver the Israelites, was rescued from death and brought up in the courts of Pharaoh himself.

When Pharaoh enslaved the Israelites, God sent Moses to demand that Israel be set free. Pharaoh refused. But the more Pharaoh hardened his heart, the more God made a name for himself. The result was that at Mount Sinai the nation of Israel was formed as a kingdom of priests, who were to be wholly consecrated to the service of God[4]. The Exodus was a wonderful fulfillment of God's promise to Abraham. There may have been 2 million people whom the Lord rescued from slavery in Egypt.

The Prediction of Blessing and Judgment

Near the end of the wilderness wandering, Moses predicted that God would bless his people but that they would not obey him. They would follow after other gods. Because of this, they would receive the curses of the covenant. After they had received both blessings and judgment they would return to the LORD.

God did bless his people. He sent judges to defend them and take care of them. But they rejected the Lord, who handed them over to the Philistines[5]. Then it's as if he awakened from sleep, beat back his enemies and put his king--David--on Mount Zion[6]. Under the rule of David and Solomon, the kingdom of Israel was at its peak. It looked as if the kingdom had finally come. One of the Psalmists calls on all the nations to praise the LORD because of God's love and faithfulness to Israel.[7] It was through Israel that God would bless the nations of the world.

Because of sin, however, God had to judge his people. First, the 10 northern tribes were sent into captivity, never to return. Judah also turned away from the Lord and was eventually sent into captivity. Only a remnant returned. Even they were not faithful. How could Israel long survive this ongoing judgment?

The Suffering Servant

When Isaiah was predicting the captivity of Judah and the return of a remnant, he also spoke of the Servant of the Lord who would bring justice and light to the nations. He would bring God's salvation to the ends of the earth.[8] This Servant is none other than Israel.[9] Abraham's descendants would finally be a blessing to the world as God had promised.

At other times, however, Isaiah indicates that this Servant is an individual within Israel. He gathers the Israelites who have been scattered in judgment.[10] The nation of Israel is God's Servant, his kingdom of priests. But they aren't faithful, and they need to be judged. Finally, only one Israelite remains who can face God's judgment against his people. The Servant gathers Israel and fulfills Israel's mission by suffering on her behalf.[11]

Grace and Victory Through Judgment

Jesus was that Servant. He was also the predicted son of Adam and Eve who would both suffer and destroy the evil one. The serpent struck him. It looked as if all the hope of the disciples and of the ages had been dashed to the ground as Jesus hung on the cross. But Jesus' death turns out to the be the final and greatest blow to Satan. The evil one is finally crushed. Jesus' death is a sacrifice for the sins of his people. He is raised from the dead and so gains the victory over it for himself and for his people. The kingdom has come. This is what the prophets had foretold: the sufferings of Christ and the glories that would follow.[12]

Union with Christ in His Death and Resurrection

In Jesus the kingdom has come but there is a sense in which it doesn't come all at once. It must increase until it's time for Jesus to return in glory. Then will come the end. Until that time, we continue to walk in the way of the cross. Satan isn't especially after our children anymore. The child he was after has already come but Satan hates us because he hates Jesus, and we are united to him.

Furthermore, our union with Jesus involves union with him in both his death and resurrection. When we give ourselves to Jesus, we say we're willing to serve him unto death. At that moment we die to sin. And someday we will die physically for him. But he has taken the sting out of death, and it will result in our glorification.

Until that time, we have the privilege of suffering for Christ.[13] Furthermore, although we don't enjoy the suffering, we do rejoice in it because we know that God uses it to make us more like Jesus and more effective as agents of his kingdom.[14] In fact, he works out every-

191

thing for our good—that is, so we will become like Jesus and be more effective.[15] And the more we become like Jesus, the more we hope for that day of our glorification in which we will be made further like him because we will see him as he is.[16]

After the resurrection of Jesus, the kingdom still comes by the way of the cross in which we follow our Lord. That's why Paul says,

> .... always carrying about in the body the dying of Jesus, so that the life of Jesus also may be manifested in our body. For we who live are constantly being delivered over to death for Jesus' sake, so that the life of Jesus also may be manifested in our mortal flesh.
> 2 Corinthians 4:10-11 NASB 1995

We are united with Christ in his death. And as we experience the sufferings which point to our physical death, we also experience his life. We become more like Jesus and the kingdom comes in our own lives.

Furthermore, through our sufferings the gospel is proclaimed in all the earth. Paul says to the Colossians,

> Now I rejoice in my sufferings for your sake, and in my flesh I do my share on behalf of His body, which is the church, in filling up what is lacking in Christ's afflictions. Of this church I was made a minister according to the stewardship from God bestowed on me for your benefit....
> Colossians 1:24-25a NASB 1995

This doesn't mean that what Christ suffered on the cross wasn't enough to pay for our sins. It means that Paul walks in the way of the cross. The spread of God's kingdom is accompanied by suffering. But the suffering is "for the sake of the church." God uses the suffering we experience as a result of our union with him to further the expansion of his kingdom. Because of our union with Christ, we are willing to be servants, even if it hurts. The necessity of this servant attitude is evident in what Paul says to the church at Rome.

> Now we who are strong ought to bear the weaknesses of those without strength and not just please ourselves. Each of us is to please his neighbor for his good, to his edification. For even Christ did not please Himself.... Therefore, accept one another, just as Christ also accepted us to the glory of God. For I say that Christ has become a servant to the circumcision on behalf of the truth of God to confirm the promises given to the fathers, and for the Gentiles to glorify God for His mercy; as it is written....
>
> Romans 15:2-3a, 7-8 NASB 1995

Then he cites several passages from the Old Testament to support his argument, including Psalm 117, which was mentioned above. According to this Psalm, when the nations see the love and faithfulness of God to Israel, they also will praise him. This love and faithfulness were supremely demonstrated in the coming of the Suffering Servant. He didn't come to be served but to serve and to give his life as a ransom for many.[17] The nations come into the kingdom when Jesus comes as a servant unto death.

Paul admonishes the church at Rome to display this same servant-like attitude by accepting one another and building one another up. The kingdom comes as those who are united to Christ in his death and resurrection are willing to serve unto death. Whoever wants to be great in the kingdom of God must be the servant of all.[18] Being engaged in the mission of God requires that we be willing to die for the cause. And since we're willing to lose everything for the sake of the kingdom, we fervently pray "Thy kingdom come!"

Appendix F: Triumphalism vs. Triumph

I believe the Bible teaches that God's people are kingdom agents on a mission given to us by God. "Agent" is often defined in these two ways: (1) a person who acts on behalf of another person, and (2) someone who takes an active role in bringing about a specified effect. I believe God's people are agents in both senses. Some people think this formulation is overly optimistic, as I'll explain below

My Assumptions

Here are the main issues (and assumptions I make) involved in the following discussion:

1. God made us in his image as leaders/rulers under him to carry out his kingdom purposes in his name. This is what I call kingdom agency. It has both individual and collective aspects.
2. The relationship between God's actions and ours involves a mystery. For example, we are to work out our salvation

because it is God who works in us (Philippians 2:12).
God normally works through his people.

3. After the fall, God's plan of redemption is designed to
   deal with the fall so that he fulfills his original plan of
   creation. Our kingdom agency is continued.

4. The Bible views the relationship of our words, actions
   and character as one of integration around Christ. They
   are all equally important in our kingdom agency.

5. The individual and the collective are equally important
   in God's kingdom. This equal emphasis reflects the
   individual and collective aspects of the Trinity, which is
   equally one (collective) and many (individual).

6. There is continuity between This Age and The Age to
   Come. The latter is the glorious culmination of the
   process of "becoming" that God built into creation.[1] Our
   kingdom agency is necessary in the movement from one
   age to the other.

7. There is discontinuity between This Age and The Age to
   Come (and between the Now-But-Not-Yet and The Age
   to Come). The culmination is so much more glorious than
   the beginning that it requires the intervention of the
   Second Adam throughout history and at his second
   coming.

There is a sense in which the Bible is about the coming of God's
rule--his kingdom--to earth. Even before the fall, Adam and Eve
looked forward to a fuller manifestation of God's kingdom on earth as
God worked through their agency. They were to fill, subdue and
reign over the earth, after which the life held out as a future hope in
the Tree of Life would become a reality. They were kingdom agents
on a mission. After the fall, the challenge to the full coming of his
kingdom increased. But even now we are to pray, "Your kingdom
come, your will be done, on earth as it is in heaven."[2]

Through the agency of God's people, the Messiah was born, and it was through him that the kingdom has come--though not yet in its fullness. So, there is an important sense in which only God can bring the kingdom. It was the God-man alone who on the cross rescued his people from their sins, from death and from the power of the evil one. At the same time, God has also always worked through his people in some way, giving them a significant role in his kingdom purposes. Ruling under him is one of the ways they image him.

Faithful Witness vs. Kingdom Agent

I would like to interact with Kevin DeYoung and Greg Gilbert on this subject since they deny we are kingdom agents. They say,

> .... the disciples .....were to "witness"—not build, not establish, not usher in, not even build for the kingdom—but bear witness to it. They were to be subjects and heralds, not agents, of the kingdom. [3]

DeYoung and Gilbert contrast being a *faithful witness*[4] with being a *kingdom agent*. They are in favor of the former and against the latter. It seems to me that being a faithful witness is also part of being a kingdom agent, but for them "kingdom agent" implies too much. As a result, they want to limit our kingdom influence to the verbal proclamation of the gospel that results in conversion, discipleship and churches.[5]

Triumphalism

I think the contrast DeYoung and Gilbert make between kingdom agency and being a faithful witness reflects their legitimate concern with what I'll call "triumphalism." For example, they say,

> Sometimes people talk as if by renovating a city park or turning a housing slum into affordable, livable apartments,

we are extending God's reign over that park or that neighborhood. We're "bringing order from chaos," someone might say, and therefore expanding the kingdom.[6]

I have great expectations about the transformative influence of the gospel on the nations before the second coming of Christ. Since Jesus is the human king of the world, I expect to see the implications of the triumph of the king—the triumph he gained through his death and resurrection—worked out through his providential intervention and through his people. Triumphalism--as I see it--typically assumes a kind of kingdom agency that, step by step in an ever-upward linear fashion, stamps out all the effects of the fall—usually by imposing itself through government—until by the time Christ comes again, everything is pretty much already taken care of. In other words, triumphalism is overly optimistic about the scope and effectiveness of our kingdom agency to bring the fullness of the kingdom of God and de-emphasizes the transformative role of Christ's intervention in history—even through seeming setbacks— including his second coming.

However, the kingdom does not always come in the kind of linear fashion that triumphalists often expect.[7] In addition, triumphalism often minimizes the greatness of God's plans for his kingdom. The glory that awaits us is much greater than what results from bringing order out of chaos or lessening the effects of sin in a given situation. God's plan is not a mere return to Eden, but something much more glorious that could only come about through the intervention of the King at his second coming.

The concern of DeYoung and Gilbert is that Christians are getting sidetracked into focusing on programs for alleviating poverty and otherwise transforming society in ways that overlook evangelism and the conversion of the lost, and in ways that overlook the great discontinuity between life in the Now But Not Yet and life in the Age to Come after Christ's second coming. They encourage Christians to help others and do good deeds, but they insist that *the mission of the church* is limited to the *proclamation* of the gospel. They refer to the Great Commission as expressing this priority. Helping others is good and we should do it, but proclaiming the gospel is our mission as a church and is more important. Another reason for this posture is that they want to avoid the sense of guilt that comes with realizing there are still poor people on earth, people are still suffering, and so on, and "what are you doing about it?"[8] If our mission is to eliminate all the effects of sin so that the kingdom comes in its fullness, then we should be greatly involved in culture transforming activities. So, in their attempt to combat triumphalism, DeYoung and Gilbert end up limiting our role in God's kingdom to proclamation--to verbal communication. For them, this means we are not to see ourselves as kingdom agents, but as heralds and faithful witnesses.

Transformational Kingdom Activity

I understand and agree with the desire of DeYoung and Gilbert to combat triumphalism. However, I disagree with their assessment on two levels. First, I don't think the Great Commission is meant to be viewed as only verbal/proclamation. We are not just to *teach* people, but to teach them *to obey*. Surely this involves modeling what the teaching looks like. Faith without works is dead. Actions that model and incarnate what we teach must be part of the mission of the church. Furthermore, the Great Commission includes baptizing people into the name of the Trinity. This involves a relationship between them and God on the one hand, and between them and God's people on the other. Promoting loving relationships is surely part of the mission of the church and not incidental to it. I'm especially concerned about limiting the mission of the church to verbal proclamation because of the tendency in Reformed churches to over-depend on what we're good at--doctrine. This over emphasis ignores the covenantal relationship among our words, our actions and our character that are meant to be integrated in Christ. It puts words about Christ--rather than Christ himself--at the center of our mission.

In the second place, I disagree with their assessment because I think they over-emphasize the discontinuity mentioned above and de-emphasize the continuity. Everywhere in Scripture our actions are considered significant kingdom activity. In their commendable attempt to argue against those who over-emphasize the continuity and thus our role in the coming of the kingdom, it seems to me they end up over-emphasizing the discontinuity, and thus limit our most important kingdom influence to verbal proclamation.

Although I am against what I've called "triumphalism," I don't think that transformative activities are thereby excluded from the mission of the church, or that we should not expect to see significant progress in kingdom influence in society. The kingdom comes as Christ's reign is extended--not just among more people, but also as that reign in and among his people exerts its influence on the world. An over-focus on individual transformation that suppresses structural transformation is, I think, unbiblical. Structure refers to the ways in which people and things are related to each other and so result in either a Biblical or unbiblical whole (or more often, a mixture of biblical and unbiblical). We should seek to influence our culture in such a way that the structures of society reflect God's glory. This helps people see what the kingdom of God is supposed to look like. The individual and collective or structural are equally important in God's kingdom.

The progress that comes through our kingdom agency is often similar to the progress that occurred in Jesus' death in that it didn't *look* much like progress. We now walk the way of the cross[9]. It is in the midst of and even through our suffering and death that the Lord brings about progress in his kingdom. Sometimes we see the church in certain locations having a great impact because of Christ and his Spirit working through them, and other times we might see that same church declining in kingdom influence. But progress in the kingdom isn't always that clear to us. It is often mysterious. Sometimes we think we see it here and there, but ultimately, it's something we accept by faith. We accept it by faith because according to the parable of the leaven,[10] the kingdom *is* progressing, even if it isn't always that visible.[11] Hendriksen says,

> The point Jesus is making in this parable is this: the reign of God, introduced into human hearts and lives *from without*, once having entered, exerts a wholesome, penetrating, and transforming influence *within and from within outward*, upon hearts and lives. It leads men onward toward the goal of perfection God has set for them. In doing so, it favorably affects every sphere of life in which they move.[12]

Kingdom progress should not be viewed as triumphalistic. But the church can and should make progress in its mission, which includes not only verbal proclamation, but also the incarnation of the message of the gospel in such a way that the church functions as salt and light in the culture. What I see in Scripture is that proclamation is meaningful primarily in the context of biblical deeds and character. People understand what you mean by your words when you live it out in practical ways. God always accompanies his words with deeds, and so should we. The mission of the church cannot be reduced to words. As Hendriksen says,

> [The Christian's] purpose is not merely to get to heaven when he dies, or only to be an instrument in God's hand to bring others there, but everywhere to bring every thought of whatever kind into submission to, and therefore harmony with, the mind and will of Christ (see 2 Cor. 10:5), that is, to demand that not only every tongue but also every "domain of life" shall exalt him. Therefore Christ's true follower actively promotes such causes as the abolition of slavery, the restoration of women's rights, the alleviation of poverty, the repatriation, if practicable, of the displaced (if not practicable then help of some other kind), the education of the illiterate, the reorientation of fine arts along Christian lines, etc. He

promotes honesty among those who govern and those who are governed, as well as in business, industry, and commerce. He does all this not apart from but in connection with, in fact as part and parcel of, the evangelization of the world.[13]

The full coming of the kingdom requires the second coming of Christ. But that doesn't make our actions insignificant for its coming. In fact, our actions--specifically prayers and holy living are mentioned--can speed up[14] the progress and coming of the kingdom. We are called to do what we can to show what we believe by what we do. Somehow, even in the midst of weakness and failure, God uses that missional activity to move forward his kingdom purposes. What specifically you or your church will do depends largely on your gifts and the situation in which you find yourself. But incarnating our words is part of the mission of the church. And when people believe, it makes a difference.

I think it's biblical to talk about "transformation" in the context of the mission of the church. But transformation should not be interpreted in the context of triumphalism. Rather, I suggest understanding transformation in light of the seven assumptions with which I began.

As believers, we are to stop allowing ourselves to be *fashioned* by the pattern of this evil age. Rather, we should be *transformed* by the renewing of our mind--which in this case refers to our inner being: the heart.[15] Some might say this transformation is not part of our mission, although it is something we should do. It's hard for me to make sense of that idea. It separates what we say from what we do and who we are. The biblical view of the integration of words, actions and character around Christ keeps me from reducing the mission of the church to verbal proclamation. Our mission involves proclamation with a view to the transformation of the people around us--as we ourselves experience that transformation--so that God's reign is increasingly manifest. We should long for our neighbors and the people in our country to see the transformation that happens when people believe and live out of the gospel. It has an impact. Hendriksen says,

> That this "yeast" of the rule of Christ in human hearts, lives, *and spheres* has already exerted a wholesome influence in thousands of ways, and that this influence is still continuing, is clear to all who have eyes to see. All one has to do is to compare conditions—for example, the treatment of prisoners of war, of women, of workmen, of the underprivileged—in countries where Christ's rule has not yet become acknowledged to any great extent, with those existing in nations where this principle has already been operative for some time on a generous scale.[16]

I have seen people proclaim the gospel in a truthful way, but also in a way that is so decontextualized and dis-incarnated that it actually pushes people away from the kingdom instead of extending it even numerically. Yet the people involved in ministry were proclaiming the gospel without verbal error. Were they carrying out the mission of the church? Were they doing so effectively? The mission of the church should not be reduced to verbal proclamation. It should include striving toward the transformation of ourselves and of those around us--including societal structures. Whatever the discontinuity between this Now-But-Not-Yet time and the final stage of the kingdom, there is continuity between our missional efforts and that final expression just as there is continuity between the natural body we received at creation and the spiritual[17] body we will receive at Christ's second coming.[18]

Belief and Unbelief

It seems to me that DeYoung and Gilbert encourage us not to expect much until the second coming. They say,

I know you have big plans and dreams. That's good. Really it is. But big plans are only accomplished after many days and years of small things. What I'm trying to say is, pray for the extraordinary, but expect the ordinary.[19]

There is a sense in which I can agree with this statement. God often accomplishes his great purposes in and through ordinary situations in life--and in ways that are not spectacular. But it sounds like they are saying, "God isn't really doing too much through you. So don't get your expectations up. Pray for the extraordinary, because God has promised great things. But don't expect much to happen--maybe not until Christ returns. That's when he will fulfill his great promises." What I have noticed in the church is that most people--even those who know his great promises--don't really expect God to do much here and now. Maybe someday and in far off lands, but not in my city, my church and my life. I call that unbelief. In their attempt to combat triumphalism, do DeYoung and Gilbert end up actually encouraging the unbelief that is so prevalent in the church?

Since Jesus is now the human king of the world, I expect him to do great things. Can't we be stirred to believe that God will do and is doing great things through his people as we faithfully serve him[20] even though we may never in this life be famous or recognized for it--even though it may take eyes of faith to see God at work fulfilling his promises and bringing the fullness of his kingdom?

What I see in the Bible is that we his people are kingdom agents sent on a mission, and that he uses our words, as well as our *actions and character*--in ways that aren't always clear to us--to bring the fullness of his kingdom. We are kingdom agents in word, deed and loving presence, not *merely* heralds. That is very exciting.

Appendix G: Toward a Theology of Sleep and Night

Introduction

Sleep often seems very strange to me--as well as a waste of time. So much more could be accomplished if we didn't have to sleep. Don't get me wrong--I enjoy a good night's sleep. But that's because I get tired. If we didn't get tired we could get a lot more done. Why did God create us with a need to sleep? Why did he create night?

The Perspective of Creation/Eschaton

The night-day cycle--and the sleep that night affords--are not a result of the fall. They are built into God's very good creational plan for mankind.

God's plan has two stages: (1) This Age and (2) The Age to Come.[1] The former is characterized by the night-day cycle. In the Age to Come, on the other hand, there will be no night. The night-day cycle is transformed into continuous day.

The sun shall be no more your light by day, nor for brightness shall the moon give you light; but the Lord will be your everlasting light, and your God will be your glory. Your sun shall no more go down, nor your moon withdraw itself; for the Lord will be your everlasting light....

Isaiah 60:19-20 ESV

And the city has no need of sun or moon to shine on it, for the glory of God gives it light, and its lamp is the Lamb.

Revelation 21:23 ESV

And night will be no more. They will need no light of lamp or sun, for the Lord God will be their light, and they will reign forever and ever.

Revelation 22:5 ESV

In This Age our bodies receive energy from the sun. But that energy is not enough to keep us going continually. We need to sleep at night in order to recuperate our strength. In the Age to Come God's people will have Spirit-controlled bodies.[2] These bodies will be so controlled and energized by the Spirit of God that they will not need to sleep.

The night-day cycle, then, points us to the transitory and preparatory nature of This Age. You might say it's the caterpillar stage of God's plan, while the Age to Come is the butterfly stage. Even apart from the fall there is a sense in which This Age is weak: it requires the recuperation of strength through sleep.[3] The "weakness" of This Age is meant to be a constant reminder of the greater glory of the Age to Come. Even before the fall, mankind were designed to live in hope of this greater glory to come.

Effects of the Fall

The rebellion of Adam and Eve was in effect an absolutization of This Age, disconnecting it from the Age to Come. They wanted the greater glory of the Age to Come "now," and they wanted to have it within This Age. They didn't want to go through the preparatory stage. This meant that mankind lost the hope of arriving at the Eternal Day. Night becomes permanent instead of a transitory pointer to a greater Age. Sin, then, becomes associated with night. Instead of sleeping at night to recuperate strength in hope of the eternal day, sinful man works during the night to hide his sin.

> .... men of perverted speech, who forsake the paths of upright-
> ness to walk in the ways of darkness....
> *Proverbs 2:11-13 ESV*
> And this is the judgment: the light has come into the
> world, and people loved the darkness rather than the light
> because their works were evil. For everyone who does wicked
> things hates the light and does not come to the light, lest his
> works should be exposed.
> *John 3:19-20 ESV*

In a fallen world, eventually the darkness will overtake the day. This Age becomes the domain of darkness.

> We must work the works of him who sent me while it is day;
> night is coming, when no one can work.
> *John 9:4 ESV*

Redemption

However, the Lord Jesus has delivered his people from the domain of darkness and has transferred us into the Age to Come--in a now-but-not-yet fashion.

> He has delivered us from the domain of darkness and trans-
> ferred us to the kingdom of his beloved Son....
> *Colossians 1:13 ESV*

As a result, believers in Christ are no longer citizens of the night, but of the day.

> For you are all children of light, children of the day. We are not of the night or of the darkness.
> *1 Thessalonians 5:5 ESV*

Therefore we should be very careful not to be lulled to sleep by the lures of the night. We must resist--through the means of grace-- the evil/night forces that want to captivate us and make us citizens of the night.

> So then let us not sleep, as others do, but let us keep awake and be sober.
> *1 Thessalonians 5:6 ESV*
> Jesus answered, "Are there not twelve hours in the day? If anyone walks in the day, he does not stumble, because he sees the light of this world. But if anyone walks in the night, he stumbles, because the light is not in him."
> *John 11:9-10 ESV*

Conclusion

The night-day cycle was designed to point us to God's two-stage design. We were designed to live in hope of a greater glory to come. After the fall, the evil one became the god of This Age.[4] This launching stage had become disconnected from the final goal. It had become an end in itself--destined to end in eternal night.

But God in Christ has delivered us from this domain of darkness and has transferred us into the Age to Come which is characterized by eternal day. We are even now citizens of the Age to Come but sill have a mission to complete within This Age--announcing God's terms of surrender to his enemies who live in darkness.

Notes

Preface

1. To give you an idea of my theological orientation, I am firmly planted within the Kuyperian and Van Tillian theological tradition that emphasizes the Lordship of Christ over all of creation and the current reign of Christ in the Now-But-Not-Yet kingdom. I believe the Bible encourages optimism about what Jesus Christ the King will do through his current reign, even while I hold firmly to the reality of our current walk along the way of the cross. The advance of the kingdom and increasing persecution are not incompatible. In fact, that's what we see today.

1. Pray for the Kingdom

1. The NASB 1995 says "the gospel of God," but still goes on to say that his message centered around the kingdom of God.
2. Some who hold a premillennial position deny that Jesus is now reigning as king. They believe that such a reign is reserved for a 1000-year reign prior to the final judgment. To those who hold this premillennial position, I recommend George Eldon Ladd's premillennial position that still affirms the present reign of Christ. You can find a later reprint here: My Book
3. As well as divine!
4. Peter made this clear in his sermon on the day of Pentecost. In this sermon (see Acts 2:29-36), Peter had just quoted Psalm 16:8-11, including a promise God had made to David in verse 10. He said, "You will not leave my soul in Hades, nor will you allow your Holy One to see corruption." Peter explains that this refers to David's greater son Jesus Christ. The promise was fulfilled in the resurrection of Christ.[1] Peter goes on to quote from Psalm 110:1, in which the Father ("the Lord") promised the Christ ("my Lord") that he would sit at the Father's right hand. In other words, he would be the human king of the world sitting on the throne of David.
5. Of course, he died in the place of the elect only. But he sincerely offers forgiveness to all according to John 3:16.
6. Romans 5:12-18. One the one hand, Jesus as the Second Adam represents his people—those who receive grace and trust in him. But since everyone is sincerely offered the opportunity to repent, there is a sense in which Jesus as the Second Adam is the head of the whole human race.
7. Of course, God is always king over all, but Adam and Eve—designated by God to be rulers under him, fell into the hands of the evil one by sinning against God. The Old Testament records the emergence of great empires that ruled–if not the whole known world–much of it. In one of his visions, Daniel saw the following

empires: Babylon, Persia, Greece and Rome. For the most part they were ruled by demons. Then Daniel saw the kingdom of God crushing all of them and bringing the kingdom of God. Paul says in 2 Corinthians 4:4 that Satan is "the god of this age." However, because Jesus has brought the eschatological kingdom, "this age" has no future. It is destined to perish.

8. Colossians 1:13-14
9. See Appendix G.
10. Therefore, since the children share in flesh and blood, He Himself likewise also partook of the same, so that through death He might destroy the one who has the power of death, that is, the devil, and free those who through fear of death were subject to slavery all their lives. Hebrews 2:14-15 NASB 1995
11. See 2 Corinthians 5:18-20. I am indebted to Richard Pratt for this helpful and Biblical phrase.
12. Of course, no one is able to accept his terms of surrender without his sovereign regenerating grace.
13. 2 Corinthians 4:4 NKJV
14. These two dimensions or realms correspond to what the Bible calls "this age" and "the age to come." However, "this age" was created good as a kind of launching pad for "the age to come." It only became the domain of darkness after the fall. And even then, there was some light as God worked through his people.
15. God's creational plan included two ages, which the Bible calls "This Age" and "The Age to Come." (See below.) This Age was to be a kind of launching pad for the Age to Come. It wasn't designed to last forever. When the evil one became the god of This Age through Adam's sin, he gained authority over an age that was destined to fall away once the Age to Come arrived. While believers still live within "This Age" and have a mission within it, we are not under the authority of the evil one.
16. Your kingdom come, your will be done on earth as it is in heaven. Matthew 6:10 NASB 1995
17. My examples are drawn from real experiences and situations but are written in such a way that identities are not revealed.
18. Matthew 13:31-33
19. 2 Corinthians 4:7-11
20. Steven J. Lawson, *The Evangelistic Zeal of George Whitefield*, Reformation Trust, 2013. p. 21.
21. The Bible does teach that in general, obedience results in blessing—often including good circumstances. But in a fallen world, these are mixed with challenging circumstances. See Appendix D for reasons why God's people suffer.
22. Revelation 21:4
23. This is not to suggest that food is only utilitarian. The chief end of man, according to the Westminster Catechism, is to glorify God *and* enjoy him forever. Part of enjoying God is enjoying his creation, including good food. But in the Lord's Prayer, the focus seems to be on food as a means to serve in the kingdom.
24. And very possibly personal prayers. See Appendix A.
25. I believe this is how we should interpret Paul's prayer to be healed. He asked to be healed because he thought being healed would allow him to be more effective as a kingdom agent. Jesus did answer his prayer. "You want to be more effective? My power is made perfect in weakness." 2 Corinthians 12:7-10

2. Pray as a Kingdom Agent

1. See Appendix F for my discussion with some who don't like to view Christians as kingdom agents.
2. Open Theism denies that God knows everything. They affirm that if he did, there's no way man could be responsible for his actions. Hyper-Calvinism, on the other hand, downplays the significance of our actions in an attempt to preserve God's sovereignty. See my further comments on this subject in Appendix C.
3. See 1 Kings 22:34. "Now one man drew his bow at random and struck the king of Israel in a joint of the armor." (NASB 1995) From a human perspective this was a random event, but God was clearly at work in it for his purposes.
4. According to fatalism, it doesn't matter what you do or don't do. Everything is going to happen the way it's going to happen, and our actions are irrelevant to the outcome.
5. In this statement I am influenced by Harvie Conn, my adviser for my doctoral work at Westminster Theological Seminary. In particular, see *Evangelism: Doing Justice and Preaching Grace.* (Zondervan: 1982) See especially chapter 5.
6. Philippians 1:19
7. This is the King James translation. Of this interpretation Hendriksen says, "This translation is acceptable as long as the concept of equal partnership is ruled out. God and man are never equals in the proclamation of the gospel, for man is merely an instrument in God's hand and works not next to him but for him. (Kistemaker, S. J., & Hendriksen, W. [1953-2001]. *Vol. 18: Exposition of the First Epistle to the Corinthians.* New Testament Commentary (107). Grand Rapids: Baker Book House.) By putting it this way, I'm emphasizing one aspect of our relationship to Christ. But I think it's an aspect that has been somewhat overlooked in my circles.
8. Of course, in another sense, he definitely tells us what to do. But as we walk within his revealed will, he wants to know how we would like his help.
9. Of course he would, because he's the one who gave these to them.
10. Hendriksen, W., & Kistemaker, S. J. (1953-2001). *Vol. 1-2: Exposition of the Gospel According to John.* New Testament Commentary (Jn 14:13–14). Grand Rapids: Baker Book House. Hendriksen, W., & Kistemaker, S. J. (1953-2001). *Vol. 1-2: Exposition of the Gospel According to John.* New Testament Commentary (Jn 14:13–14). Grand Rapids: Baker Book House.

3. Pray as an Adventurer

1. Tolkien, J. R. R. (1954). The Lord of the Rings. London,, Allen & Unwin.
2. Genesis 1:2, John 1:1-3
3. Genesis 1:3-separates light from darkness, Genesis 1:7-separates water from water, Genesis 1:9-gathered waters.
4. Genesis 1:3-light, Genesis 1:6-expanse, Genesis 1:14-lights, Genesis 1:21-living things of the sea and birds, Genesis 1:25-land animals, Genesis 1:27-man.
5. Genesis 1:11-the land produces vegetation, Genesis 1:20-the sea produces living creatures, Genesis 1:24-the land produces living creatures.
6. Genesis 1:18-the lights govern the day and night.

7. Genesis 1:22-fish and birds, Genesis 1:28-man.
8. They also reflect him in other ways, but these are most obvious in the passage. Their ruling, forming and filling is done on a creaturely level.
9. That is, after God's forming and filling during 6 days.
10. In Hebrew: "kabash." R. Laird Harris, Gleason L. Archer, Jr., Bruce K. Waltke. *Theological Wordbook of the Old Testament.* Vol 1. p. 430.
11. *Theological Wordbook of the Old Testament.* p. 430.
12. As God was with mankind in the Garden before the fall.
13. John Frame, *The Doctrine of the Knowledge of God: A Theology of Lordship* (Phillipsburg, New Jersey: Presbyterian and Reformed Publishing House, 1987), pp. 15-18. Frame shows that it is God's authority, control and presence that best summarize the concept of divine lordship.
14. In John 5, Jesus healed a man on the sabbath. The Jewish leaders accuse him of wrongdoing. His response indicates that they had misunderstood the meaning of the sabbath. The sabbath is not about idleness. Jesus said to them, "My Father is working until now, and I myself and working." (John 5:17 NASB 1995)
15. Colossians 2:16-17, Hebrews 10:1
16. 1 Peter 5:8
17. I owe this helpful phrase to Richard Pratt.
18. Romans 8:17, 1 Corinthians 3:21
19. 2 Corinthians 5:16-20
20. James 4:7
21. John 2:11
22. "according to the flesh" 2 Corinthians 5:16
23. Matthew 27:18, John 12:19
24. Acts 2:23, 4:27-28
25. John 1:29
26. Luke 9:23
27. The new creation refers both to the individual who is regenerated and whose identity is now "in Christ," but also to the believer's participation in the wider reality of God's kingdom.
28. Written by Baroness Orczy, published in 1905.
29. 1 Corinthians 3:22
30. Hebrews 4:9

4. Pray as a Warrior

1. Now it's very sad to see the sharply declining influence of the gospel on my home culture.
2. Peretti, Frank E., Crossway Books, 1986.
3. Peretti, Frank E., Crossway Books, 1989.
4. 2 Kings 6:17
5. From an unknown Greek source. Translated by John Mason Neale, 1862
6. 1 Peter 5:8. This is also a reference to C. S. Lewis' *The Screwtape Letters.* "To us a human is primarily food; our aim is the absorption of its will into ours, the increase

of our own area of selfhood at its expense." Lewis, C. S.. *The Screwtape Letters* (p. 38). HarperCollins. Kindle Edition.

7. From *A Mighty Fortress is our God* (Ein feste Burg ist unser Gott) written by Martin Luther between 1527 and 1529.
8. Ephesians 6:12
9. From *A Mighty Fortress is our God* (Ein feste Burg ist unser Gott) written by Martin Luther between 1527 and 1529.
10. From *A Mighty Fortress is our God* (Ein feste Burg ist unser Gott) written by Martin Luther between 1527 and 1529.
11. Here I follow Hendriksen, W., & Kistemaker, S. J. (1953-2001). Vol. 7: *Exposition of Ephesians. New Testament Commentary* (271–272). Grand Rapids: Baker Book House.
12. Matthew 4:6
13. Matthew 4:6. See also Antonio, A Merchant of Venice who says, "The devil can quote Scripture to his purpose." Shakespeare, *The Merchant of Venice* I.iii.v.95
14. 2 Corinthians 11:14
15. Genesis 3:5
16. John 8:44
17. For example, Peter denied he even knew Jesus when Jesus submitted to the local authorities taking him to trial. (Matthew 26:69-75).
18. For example, God gave Solomon great wisdom and many other blessings. People came from all over to hear his wisdom. But he married many unbelieving wives and they turned his heart away from the Lord. (1 Kings 11)
19. Ephesians 6:24, James 4:7
20. Hendriksen, W., & Kistemaker, S. J. (1953-2001). Vol. 7: *Exposition of Ephesians. New Testament Commentary* (271). Grand Rapids: Baker Book House.
21. Every culture has what I call a point system by which it judges your worth. I will explain this in greater detail in chapter 5.
22. Hendriksen, W., & Kistemaker, S. J. (1953-2001). *Vol. 7: Exposition of Ephesians.* New Testament Commentary (274). Grand Rapids: Baker Book House.
23. Of course, not everything that comes to one's mind is necessarily from the Lord. It must be examined in light of Scripture and in light of your current spiritual condition. Do you have a good conscience before the Lord?
24. Hendriksen, W., & Kistemaker, S. J. (1953-2001). *Vol. 7: Exposition of Ephesians.* New Testament Commentary (281). Grand Rapids: Baker Book House.
25. In this regard, see similar ideas in Richard Pratt's book, *Pray With Your Eyes Open.* (P&R Publishing, 1999)
26. 1 Timothy 4:7
27. Our bodies are the temple of the Holy Spirit, and he gives his loves ones sleep. 1 Corinthians 6:19-20, Psalm 127:2

5. Pray with Audacity

1. See *Paul: An Outline of His Theology*, by Herman Ridderbos, Grand Rapids: Wm. B. Eerdmans Publishing Company, 1975. See especially sections 11, 16, 17, 19 and 78. Ridderbos puts "flesh" in a redemptive-historical context.

2. Jesus says "this mountain," no doubt referring to Mount Moriah on which Solomon built the temple (2 Chronicles 3:3). In 70 AD, Jesus the king came to destroy the temple through the armies of Rome, thus punishing Israel for having rejected him as their Messiah and opening the way for the expansion of his kingdom through the church.
3. See also Isaiah 49:11
4. Translation by Hendriksen, W., & Kistemaker, S. J. (1953-2001). Vol. 7: *Exposition of Ephesians. New Testament Commentary* (175). Grand Rapids: Baker Book House.
5. Hendriksen, W., & Kistemaker, S. J. (1953-2001). Vol. 7: *Exposition of Ephesians. New Testament Commentary* (175). Grand Rapids: Baker Book House.

6. Pray with Boldness

1. Some sources say he was the third martyr. But Thomas Quinton Stow says "As Bishop Hooper was burnt on the morning of the same day, which was the 9th of February, 1555, it is probable that Dr. Taylor was the fourth martyr of this reign." Stow, Thomas Quinton. Memoirs of Rowland Taylor. 1833. Kessinger Legacy Reprints.
2. Of course, Henry VIII had ulterior motives in his desire to break with Rome
3. Taylor was married to Margaret Tyndale, a niece of William Tyndale, who worked tirelessly to translate the New Testament (and much of the Old) into English so people could read for themselves what it said. Tyndale was put to death as a heretic in 1536.
4. Stow, Thomas Quinton. Memoirs of Rowland Taylor. 1833. Kessinger Legacy Reprints. pp. 66-67.
5. Stow, Thomas Quinton. Memoirs of Rowland Taylor. 1833. Kessinger Legacy Reprints. p. 120.
6. Stow, Thomas Quinton. Memoirs of Rowland Taylor. 1833. Kessinger Legacy Reprints. pp. 230-231.
7. Stow, Thomas Quinton. Memoirs of Rowland Taylor. 1833. Kessinger Legacy Reprints. p. 113.
8. Stow, Thomas Quinton. Memoirs of Rowland Taylor. 1833. Kessinger Legacy Reprints. p. 235.
9. "He spake many notable things to the sheriff and yeomen of the guard that conducted him, and often moved them to weep, through his much earnest calling upon them to repent, and to amend their evil and wicked living. Oftentimes also he caused them to wonder and rejoice, to see him so constant and steadfast, void of all fear, joyful in heart, and glad to die."

    Foxe, John. *Foxe's Book of Marytrs*: Complete with Arts, Portraits, Pictures, Illustrations with Biography of John Foxe: Spirituality (Christian Classics). Kindle Edition.
10. Stow, Thomas Quinton. Memoirs of Rowland Taylor. 1833. Kessinger Legacy Reprints. p. 117, quoting Foxes' Book of Martyrs.
11. Luke 22:42
12. Literally, "work a work"

13. This is how John Calvin interprets this verse, along with many others. Some say the reaction in the verse refers to the vision of God's mighty acts in Habakkuk 3:3-15, but I don't think so.

14. See Appendix D.

15. "circumcised the eighth day, of the nation of Israel, of the tribe of Benjamin, a Hebrew of Hebrews; as to the Law, a Pharisee; as to zeal, a persecutor of the church; as to the righteousness which is in the Law, found blameless." NASB 1995

16. Acts 16:37-38, Acts 22:25-28, Acts 25

17. While it is not sinful to have points, it is sinful to live by those points.

18. There are various interpretations of this verse. For example, "fame" could be "report," and "awe" could be "fear." There are other variations as well. For a very different view, which I don't use, see O. Palmer Robertson's *The Books of Nahum, Habakkuk and Zephaniah* (Eerdmans, 1990). I think the interpretation I'm following here doesn't miss the main message that Habakkuk wants to communicate.

19. That this section is part of the prayer that began in 3:1 is evident by its title in 3:1 and by the fact that the whole chapter is enclosed by instructions for use in worship. Furthermore, it's not uncommon for a prayer to move between first and third person. See, for example, Psalms 90, 102 and 142.

20. Deuteronomy 28:13-44

21. See Appendix E.

22. Christ's "session" refers to his sitting down at the right hand of the Father. According to the book of Hebrews, Jesus sat down for several reasons: 1) because he finished his work (10:11-14), 2) because the Father approved is work (12:2), 3) to pray for his people (7:23-25), 4) because he's waiting for the right time to put an end to the suffering caused by the evil one (10:12-13) and 5) to give us a sure anchor in the ups and downs of life (6:17-20).

7. Pray with Humility

1. I'm certainly not against sharing with others examples of my own sin, but this should be done with wisdom—in ways appropriate to the particular situation—and not as a way of making people feel less spiritual for not sharing everything.

2. In spite of my poor motives for spending so much time in my daily devotions, the Lord ended up using it for my good.

3. 2 Corinthians 13:5

4. Suzanne Collins, Scholastic Press, 2008

5. The epilogue at the end of book 3 does little to change this view. If anything, it promotes a kind of balance view.

6. I recognize that many Christians use the word "balance" without meaning "the mean between the extremes." I think what they mean to communicate is that somehow two seemingly contradictory actions or attitudes come together in the Christian life in a mysterious way. However, I try to avoid using the word balance to describe these mysterious interactions because of the way people in my culture

are likely to misinterpret my words as a kind of mean between the extremes that we can accomplish by studiously emphasizing both in equal amounts.

7. Hendriksen, W., & Kistemaker, S. J. (1953-2001). Vol. 8: *Exposition of Galatians. New Testament Commentary* (234). Grand Rapids: Baker Book House.
8. Psalm 7:3-5
9. Sanderson, John, *The Fruit of the Spirit*, the Zondervan Corporation, Grand Rapids: 1977.
10. "Will I come across as proud?"
11. Ephesians 3:17-19
12. Romans 7:14ff

8. Pray Earnestly

1. Matthew 13:44-45
2. The author of Hebrews here uses a Greek word that is also used in 1 Timothy 4:6-10. The word "train" in these passages is the same one used of training in the Greek gym in which people would train to become excellent runners, wrestlers and so on. Paul connects Timothy's knowledge of the value of physical training to the greater value of spiritual training. In both cases you keep your eye on the goal, you work hard, you push yourself to excel. Paul calls it "toiling" and "striving." Of course, spiritual discipline is of much greater value because it holds promise for the present life and also for the life to come. So, Paul wants Timothy—and us—to "gymnasticize" spiritually. He wants us to work out spiritually—to discipline ourselves for godliness.
3. It isn't necessarily wrong to ask for alleviation of the pain or hardship. Paul pleaded with God for alleviation in 2 Corinthians 12:1-10. But God said no, and it was more important for Paul to have Christ's power resting upon him than to have the hardship taken away. In any case, I suspect that Paul asked for alleviation of the problem at least partly because he thought it would make him a more effective kingdom agent. To the extent that such is the case, God answered the intent of his prayer.
4. Conn, Harvie M., *Evangelism: Doing Justice and Preaching Grace*, P&R Publishing, Phillipsburg, NJ, 1982, p. 87. This is a reference to Wells, David F., "Prayer: Rebelling Against the Status Quo," *Christianity Today* vol 23, no. 25 (November 2, 1979), pp. 32-34.
5. Luke 11:13
6. 1 Kings 19:1-9

9. Pray in Ministry

1. Figure 8 is not meant to communicate that prayer is more important than the other aspects of the ministry of the church. It's in the middle because I'm highlighting it.
2. Luke 6:12-13
3. See chapter 1.

4. Of course, individual prayer is important. I'm talking here about a distortion of individual prayer.
5. See Chapter 10.
6. A philosophy of ministry has a lot to do with the "personality" of the church.
7. This is an application of Van Til's Standard, Motive and Goal/Purpose of ethics. It seems to me that John Frame's tri-perspectival approach is related to this triad of Van Til. See Van Til, *Christian Theistic Ethics* (Copyright, den Dulk Christian Foundation, 1971) pp. 1-3.
8. Of course it's good to be sensitive to those who live in the context of the church. It's important to know them—their fears, their dreams, and their tendencies to idolatry. A seeker-driven church appeals to the idolatries of the context and implies it can satisfy them.
9. Of course, most churches will also be involved in supporting cross-cultural mission —and even this should be in line with their giftedness as a church. It's nevertheless true that every church should be primarily focused on ministering to and within the specific context that is determined by their location in the world.
10. Of course, God eventually heals all his people of all our diseases. The only unknown is whether it will be now, later or at his second coming.
11. The church has grown up in many places in the world. But it has also disappeared in many places. The church in Ephesus was once thriving. In Revelation 2 Jesus commended them for many things, but also warned them that they had left their first love. Today Asia Minor has very few Christians. Why does this happen? I believe one of the reasons is that the church in a given place tends to be unaware of its own tendencies toward cultural idolatry. If churches from different cultures would learn from each other, they would be less likely to succumb to their tendencies to idolatry.

10. Pray Together

1. See also Hendriksen, W., & Kistemaker, S. J. (1953-2001). *Vol. 9: Exposition of the Gospel According to Matthew.* New Testament Commentary (702). Grand Rapids: Baker Book House.
2. Genesis 11:6
3. That is, the work of Christ through the Holy Spirit does much more than return us to an Edenic state. Rather, Christ through the gift of the Spirit brings us into the glory of the higher life anticipated in the Tree of Life and the Sabbath.
4. My examples are drawn from real experiences and situations but are written in such a way that identities are not revealed.
5. My examples are drawn from real experiences and situations but are written in such a way that identities are not revealed.
6. According to Luke 11:4, we are in no condition to accept God's forgiveness through Christ if we have an unforgiving spirit.
7. This is what the Lord Almighty says: "Many peoples and the inhabitants of many cities will yet come, and the inhabitants of one city will go to another and say, 'Let us go at once to entreat the Lord and seek the Lord Almighty. I myself am

going.' And many peoples and powerful nations will come to Jerusalem to seek the Lord Almighty and to entreat him."

8. "An Humble Attempt to Promote Explicit Agreement and Visible Union of God's People in Extraordinary Prayer for the Revival of Religion and the Advancement of Christ's Kingdom on Earth." *The Works of Jonathan Edwards*, Volume 2, (Hendrickson Publishers, 2005)

9. *The Works of Jonathan Edwards*, Volume 2, p. 311

10. Ephesians 3:17-19

11. Who knew that the Sociology of Knowledge discipline was around in Paul's day!

12. I'm not talking about differences that would change the basic message of the gospel, but important nuances that can enrich our understanding of the deep and wide implications of the gospel.

13. That is, we make an idol out of our cultural perspective.

14. And, according to some, bringing down the power of demonic forces.

15. As we read Scripture together, minister together and pray together.

16. My position on cultural bias and the importance of a diversity of perspectives is very different from that of Critical Race Theory, which frames the issues within an unbiblical worldview and thus misconstrues them. In the first place, CRT has no reason to disallow unbiblical perspectives. In the second place, CRT has no place for mutual learning through fellowship or the critique of tendencies toward idolizing otherwise legitimate perspectives. According to CRT, the dominant perspective is always a selfish grab for power and is therefore to be destroyed (by what turns out to be another selfish grab for power).

17. In his commentary on Ephesians, John Stott says, "We shall have power to comprehend these dimensions of Christ's love, Paul adds, only with all the saints. The isolated Christian can indeed know something of the love of Jesus. But his grasp of it is bound to be limited by his limited experience. It needs the whole people of God to understand the whole love of God, all the saints together, Jews and Gentiles, men and women, young and old, black and white, with all their varied backgrounds and experiences." *God's New Society: The Message of Ephesians*, InterVarsity (1979) p. 137

11. Pray with Your Spouse

1. One study showed that only 8% of Christian spouses pray together regularly.

2. There may be other reasons why couples don't pray together, but I think this is the most common.

3. In his commentary, Calvin says, "That your prayers be not hindered For God cannot be rightly called upon, unless our minds be calm and peaceable. Among strifes and contentions there is no place for prayer. Peter indeed addresses the husband and the wife, when he bids them to be at peace one with another, so that they might with one mind pray to God. But we may hence gather a general doctrine -- that no one ought to come to God except he is united to his brethren. Then as this reason ought to restrain all domestic quarrels and strifes, in order that each one of the family may pray to God; so in common life it ought to be as it were a bridle to check all contentions. For we are more than insane, if we knowingly

and wilfully close up the way to God's presence by prayer, since this is the only asylum of our salvation."

4. Kistemaker, S. J., & Hendriksen, W. (1953-2001). Vol. 16: *Exposition of the Epistles of Peter and the Epistle of Jude*. New Testament Commentary (125). Grand Rapids: Baker Book House.
5. Ephesians 5:24 This means "everything within the sphere of what is Biblical."
6. Unless, of course, the husband makes a decision that involves disobedience to the Lord.
7. Romans 8:28
8. Peter isn't saying women should be careless about how they look.
9. Matthew 11:29
10. See *The Fruit of the Spirit*, John W. Sanderson, 1977, The Zondervan Corporation. p. 125.
11. Luke 9:46-56
12. "According to knowledge" could also include the knowledge of how God made men and women. So, we could say "Christian knowledge" that interprets general revelation in light of Scripture. I think the emphasis is on having God's perspective as revealed in Scripture. See 2 Peter 1:3, where everything we need for life and godliness is given to us through our knowledge of God.
13. Proverbs 31:29
14. Of course, the stage of life you are in will have an influence on the possibilities here. If the kids are all very young, taking a walk might not be a possibility, for example.

12. Pray with Expectancy

1. Luke 1:9
2. Luke 1:12
3. Mark 9:24 NASB 1995
4. And therefore collective
5. Or maybe some form of judgment.
6. Of course, in our own strength it's impossible.
7. See Appendix B
8. Hebrews 10:11-14.
9. Hebrews 10:19-22
10. Zephaniah 3:17
11. See, for example, Acts 1:8 according to which it's the power of the Holy Spirit that enables God's people to be his witnesses throughout the world. It's true that we are not eyewitnesses of the ministry of Jesus as were the 12 apostles (Acts 1:21-22, 13:31). But we can still bear witness to the truth of the Bible and to what he has done in us. See Appendix F. See also 2 Corinthians 5:16-20 where in light of being a new creation in Christ, we are to be his ambassadors urging people to reconcile to God.
12. John 7:37ff
13. 1 Corinthians 12:7
14. Hebrews 12

15. 2 Corinthians 1:4
16. Hebrews 7:23-25
17. Romans 8:26-27
18. Hebrews 6:17-20
19. Revelation 7:9-10
20. "I understand more than the aged, Because I have observed Your precepts." Psalm 119:100 NASB 1995
21. "so that Christ may dwell in your hearts through faith; and that you, being rooted and grounded in love, may be able to comprehend with all the saints what is the breadth and length and height and depth, and to know the love of Christ which surpasses knowledge, that you may be filled up to all the fullness of God." Ephesians 3:17-19 NASB 1995
22. I try to avoid using the word "missions" because it substitutes cross-cultural mission for the mission of the church. Biblically, the former is merely a subset of the latter.
23. I'm not against giving such reports. What concerns me is the implication that sending churches have nothing to learn—apart from how little they suffer— from sister churches in other cultures. Why not ask the visiting cross-cultural missionary to preach a sermon or teach a class that highlights the things he has learned about God, the church, or the mission of the church from living and ministering in a different culture?
24. There are, in fact, Christian groups (like those who adhere to Two Kingdom theology) who admonish the church to stay in its "spiritual" lane.
25. Thankfully there are a few notable exceptions.
26. Psalm 2:7. See also Acts 2:36, 4:25, 13:33, Hebrews 1:5, 5:5, Revelation 2:26-27, 6:15-17, 11:15, and 19:15.

Appendix A: Prayer Meetings

1. Matthew 6:9-13 and Luke 11:2-4

Appendix B: Growing Your Faith

1. Matthew 13:58
2. In John 16:7 Jesus tells his disciples that it's "better" for him to go because then he will send the Holy Spirit.
3. There are others I could mention, but I think these will get you started.

Appendix C: The Use of Logic in Interpretation

1. Whether this refers to Jesus' coming in judgment in 70 AD (which in my view seems to be the case), to the second coming, or to both, the point is still the same.

2. These two errors are two examples of the theological error of not submitting one's logic to Scripture. We should certainly use our logic in our interpretation, but we should use it Biblically and not to negate one teaching because it might seem to contradict another. A second kind of theological error involves filling in the unrevealed spaces. There is a temptation to fill in the with our own imagination and thoughts the spaces that have been created by God not revealing everything to us. We don't know why he hasn't revealed everything. Filling in the space may seem logical to us. Spaces may leave what seems like an intellectual itch. But God says not to attempt to fill in the spaces. The secret to clear understanding is found in obedience. Just obey what he has revealed. A third kind of theological error is failing to love. Jesus criticized the Pharisees for making their system of theology and "obedience" more important than God and his people (Matthew 23:23-24). In many cases they did the right things, but did not love God or his people. When you disconnect obedience from love you misunderstand. When you disconnect correct concepts from love, you also misunderstand. The more you love, the more you understand. Theologians who do not love, do not understand.

Appendix D: Why Christians Suffer

1. 1 Corinthians 11
2. 1 Timothy 4:2
3. Hebrews 12
4. Romans 5:1-5
5. James 1:2-4
6. James 1:1-5
7. Hebrews 12:11 and 1 Timothy 4:6-10 use the word for exercise in the gym to describe (1) our striving to be useful in the kingdom and (2) the exercises God gives us to disciple us for godliness.
8. 2 Corinthians 1:3-7
9. James 1:12, 1 Peter 1:6
10. Hebrews 13:13, 1 Peter 4:13
11. See Chapter 3.

Appendix E: The Rebound Movement and the Way of the Cross

1. See my manuscript "Toward a Theology of Movement."
2. Imagine dropping a basketball, which then bounces up or rebounds higher than the place from which it was dropped.
3. Previous to the cross, the rebound movement focuses on the birth of godly children. Satan knows that one of them is the promised seed that is supposed to defeat him. After the cross, Satan is not so much after our children because the promised seed has already come. He hates us, however, because we are united to that Son of Man.
4. Exodus 19:6

5. Psalm 78:59
6. Psalm 78:65-70
7. Psalm 117
8. Isaiah 42:1-7, 49:6
9. Isaiah 49:3
10. Isaiah 49:5
11. Isaiah 52:13-53:12
12. 1 Peter 1:11
13. Philippians 1:29
14. Romans 5:1-5
15. Romans 8:28-29
16. Romans 5:5 and 1 John 3:2
17. Mark 10:45
18. Mark 10:44

Appendix F: Triumphalism vs. Triumph

1. This is not to imply that there will be no more "becoming" after our glorification. The second coming of Christ brings us to the close of our mission to subdue the earth.
2. Matthew 6:10
3. DeYoung, Kevin. *What Is the Mission of the Church?: Making Sense of Social Justice, Shalom, and the Great Commission* (p. 140). Crossway. Kindle Edition.
4. The word "witness" has two related meanings in the book of Acts. One is related to having been an eyewitness of Jesus' ministry. Matthias was chosen to replace Judas because he fulfilled this qualification. See Acts 1:21-22. See also Acts 13:31 where Paul and Barnabas refer to the twelve disciples as witnesses. The word "witness" can also refer to "the person who presents a testimony by which he defends and promotes a cause. (Kistemaker, S. J., & Hendriksen, W. (1953–2001). Exposition of the Acts of the Apostles (Vol. 17, p. 54). Baker Book House.)
   Of course, we can be witnesses only in the second sense.
5. How they think discipleship and churches can be limited to the verbal is beyond me.
6. DeYoung, Kevin. *What Is the Mission of the Church?: Making Sense of Social Justice, Shalom, and the Great Commission* (p. 121). Crossway. Kindle Edition.
7. See Appendix E.
8. They forget that before the flood, the world was ruled by demons. And even during the Old Testament times, demons ruled the world except in Israel (and even there the sometimes had more influence than they should have.). But now things have changed. The church has spread around the world. The evil one can no longer deceive the nations as he did in the past.
9. See Appendix E.
10. Luke 13:20-21
11. DeYoung and Gilbert interpret this parable to mean that only in the eschaton, when Christ returns, we will see progress. I have a hard time with that interpretation because in the image of leaven the process stands out.

12. Hendriksen, W., & Kistemaker, S. J. (1953–2001). *Exposition of the Gospel According to Luke* (Vol. 11, p. 704). Grand Rapids: Baker Book House.
13. Hendriksen, W., & Kistemaker, S. J. (1953–2001). *Exposition of the Gospel According to Matthew* (Vol. 9, pp. 567–568). Grand Rapids: Baker Book House.
14. 2 Thessalonians 3:1-2, 2 Peter 3:10-12
15. The word "heart" in Hebrew is the seat of the mind, the will and the emotions. According to the *Theological Wordbook of the Old Testament* (Harris, Archer and Waltke. 1980 Moody Bible Institute, pp. 466-467) the "heart" (*leb*) is "the totality of man's inner or immaterial nature...." (p. 466) "By far the majority of the usages of *leb* refer either to the inner or immaterial nature in general or to one of the three traditional personality functions of man: emotion, thought, or will." (p. 466). See also Romans 12:1-2. Hendriksen says, "the renewing of the mind, that is, not only of the organ of thinking and reasoning but of the inner disposition; better still, of the heart, the inner being". Hendriksen, W., & Kistemaker, S. J. (1953–2001). *Exposition of Paul's Epistle to the Romans* (Vol. 12–13, p. 406). Grand Rapids: Baker Book House.
16. Hendriksen, W., & Kistemaker, S. J. (1953–2001). *Exposition of the Gospel According to Matthew* (Vol. 9, p. 568). Grand Rapids: Baker Book House.
17. I take the spiritual body Paul refers to in 1 Corinthians 15 as a body completely empowered by the Spirit, and not as an immaterial body. By the way, this passage is one of the clearest showing that the incarnation is implicit in creation. (Hopefully my next book.)
18. There is also continuity between this earth and the new earth. The Greek word for "new" in Revelation 21:1 is *kainos*, which means "renewed.," not something different. See also 2 Corinthians 5:17.
19. DeYoung, Kevin. *What Is the Mission of the Church?: Making Sense of Social Justice, Shalom, and the Great Commission* (p. 261). Crossway. Kindle Edition.
20. And this is where I agree with their emphasis on being a faithful witness

Appendix G: Toward a Theology of Sleep and Night

1. See the following verses that reveal to us the Bible's two-age conception: Matthew 12:31-32, 13:38-40, 49-50, 24:3, 28:20b, Mark 10:29-30, Luke 18:29-30, 20:34-36, 1 Corinthians 2:6-8, 2 Corinthians 4:4, Galatians 1:3-5, Ephesians 1:19-21, 1 Timothy 6:17-19, Titus 2:11-14, Hebrews 6:4-7.
2. 1 Corinthians 15:35-49
3. As God created it, there is nothing sinful about This Age. Its weakness when compared to the Age to Come is not a result of sin, but points us to the need for something greater.
4. 2 Corinthians 4:4. Notice that the logic of this *Theology of Sleep and Night* points us to the subject I hope to include in my next book: that the incarnation of the Son of God (not including his suffering and death) is implicit in creation and not merely a consequence of the fall. He comes as a man to marry his bride and bring us into the Age of the Spirit. All the creation ordinances point us in this direction. Paul makes it quite explicit in 1 Corinthians 15:35-49.

About the Author

Gary Waldecker is an ordained minister in the Presbyterian Church in America. He was a cross-cultural missionary for 35 years, serving as a church planter in Chile and as an advisor to church planters in Latin America. He holds a Doctor of Ministry in Missiology from Westminster Theological Seminary in Philadelphia and a Doctor of Education in Human and Organizational Learning from The George Washington University.

https://www.garywaldecker.com
https://www.longroadpress.com

Made in the USA
Monee, IL
10 September 2023

42450356R00134